Allan McLane Hamilton

The modern Treatment of Headaches

Allan McLane Hamilton

The modern Treatment of Headaches

ISBN/EAN: 9783743340503

Manufactured in Europe, USA, Canada, Australia, Japa

Cover: Foto ©Lupo / pixelio.de

Manufactured and distributed by brebook publishing software (www.brebook.com)

Allan McLane Hamilton

The modern Treatment of Headaches

THE MODERN TREATMENT OF HEADACHES.

—BY—

ALLAN McLANE HAMILTON, M. D.

1888.
GEORGE S. DAVIS,
DETROIT, MICH.

PREFACE.

A little book of this character hardly needs a preface. I might, however, offer a word of apology for my failure to mention many remedies, which in the hands of my reader have doubtless been of great value in the treatment of this most common of ailments.

I have written these few pages, drawing from my own experience, without any great reference to other articles or books, and the remedies suggested are those in which I believe. I hope imperfect as they are, they may contain here and there a serviceable hint.

ALLAN McLANE HAMILTON.

20 East 29th St., New York.

INTRODUCTION.

HEADACHES

The complex nature of head pain must, to a great extent, affect such a thing as exactitude in diagnosis, and the multitude of immediate and remote etiological factors, and the circumstances of a modifying character in such cases, require a survey of the whole domain of disease. General symptomology must be regarded, and in but few cases can we consider headache as a distinct disorder. Head pain is external or internal, and due to a variety of influences that affect the sensory parts either of the scalp, or the contents of the cranium. Circulatory variations with resultant modifications of pressure—either hyperæmic or anæmic—the presence of toxic agents, fungus growths, transmitted irritation from remote centres, malnutrition or some grave disease of the fifth nerve; all enter in the production of this most common form of distress. No one disputes the fact that extensive disease within the skull may exist without headache. When we consider the arrangement of the skull and its soft parts, we immediately ascribe to the dura an important role as a developer of headaches. This membrane contains a large number of blood vessels and sinuses, and whenever hyperæmia, or a serious lesion is found where there are resisting bony parts, headache is almost a certainty. Many headaches, I am sure, are alone due to extra-cranial disturbances, notably scalp congestion and inflammation, and it is very probable there are headaches of an annoying character, which, as Briquet and Mills have pointed out, are simply myalgic. I am clearly of the opinion that many alleged " eye " and " uterine " headaches are ordinary myalgic affections of the temporal and occipito-frontalis muscles.

Location.—The localization of pain is of value in determining the nature of headache, but not so much as some authors would have us believe. Some years ago all vertical headaches were considered " uterine," now much sub-occipital pain is supposed to be due to pelvic disorders. There is no absolute certainty in connecting a headache with this or that bodily disorder, so far as its seat is concerned, but a study of the accompanying symptoms is of great moment, for there is after all, a more or less relative connection. It is of importance to study the time of appearance, duration, modifying influences, age of the patient, and his appearance and behavior.

The individual is very likely to be mistaken in regard to the seat of his pain, and is disposed to ascribe what may undoubtedly be a superficial pain to deeper parts. Wilks says: "I suppose that one's feelings ought not to influence the judgment, otherwise it would be thought that the pain is situated in the very depths of the brain itself. I once had an opportunity of testing the power which the individual has in discovering the seat of pain. Having scalded my head with steam rising from a pipe to vaporize a sick-room, I endeavored to analyse the character of the pain which followed, but was unable to discern how it differed in kind from the pain of ordinary headache." This is quite true, and the hyperæsthesia of many terminal filaments is quite apt to confuse the powers of space perception. An intense local pain, on the other hand, may appear to be general, as in migraine.

As I have said, the most important pathological states which are conducive to headache are those which bear relation to the condition of fulness or emptiness of the cerebral vessels. As one-fifth of all the blood in the body goes to the head, we may expect to find important disturbances in function when the amount is either greatly increased or modified. As results of cardiac excitement or disease, increased vascular tension, determinations or hyperæmic states of other organs; or exhausting fluxes; we find varieties of headache which are known as *congestive* or *anæmic*, though their distinction is by no means an arbitrary one. Certain toxic headaches belong to the first order, and neurasthenic ones to the latter. Anæmic headaches are often "uterine," and if we mingle the clinical and pathological terms we find ourselves in a helpless tangle. I prefer a different classification, which is the following:

1. Congestive headaches.
2. Anæmic headaches.

3. Organic headaches (as a rule due to structural cerebral changes).
4. Toxic headaches (*e. g.* lithæmic, uræmic, malarial, *et al.*)
5. Neuralgic headaches.
6. Neurasthenic headaches.

CHAPTER I.

CONGESTIVE HEADACHES.

Under this head come two forms: (*a*) that in which there is a general cerebral congestion and pain; (*b*) that which begins at least in one-sided pain, with lateral hyperæmia. Its forms are numerous and its causes very extensive. No age is free from it and it is perhaps the most common of all headaches. Generally speaking it is accompanied by a subjective sense of fullness, by more or lesss psychic hyperæsthesia at one time, and dulness at another; by confusion of ideas; throbbing and distension of the temporal vessels, suffusion of the skin, injection of the conjunctiva and sometimes of the sclerotics. Brilliancy of the eyes, or a lack-lustre expression, and a tendency to sleep, diffused pain, which causes the patient to declare that his head is encircled in an iron band, or that "it feels as if it would burst," are the sensorial disorders. It may occur quite suddenly in the course of an attack of indigestion, or gradually develope in the person who has suffered from obstinate constipation for a few days. In point of duration it may last for several days, or be almost continuous during the existence of an exciting cause.

In its familiar form it may result from want of sleep, a late supper, or a debauch, in which event it is often matutinal, and is associated usually with nausea and what the Germans call "katzenjammer," a sense of intolerable "seediness." The eructations or emissions from the stomach are quite apt to be intensely acid, and there is besides the diffused pain, a peculiar weight above the brows.

The treatment for such a headache is, first a good brisk saline purgative, such as Hunyadi water, Friedreichsalle, or a solution of Crab Orchard salts; a cold bath and douche, and the use of the diffusible stimulants. I have given many of my patients the following:

℞ Spts. ammon. aromatici, ℨii.
Cocæ hydrochloras, gr. x.
Ammon. bromidi., ℨiss.
Aquæ camphoræ, ad ℨiv.

M. Sig.—One teaspoonful in iced water to be repeated hourly until relief is obtained.

In some cases an aromatic bitter tonic and carminative will relieve the patient if his headache be due to alcoholic excesses:

℞ Tr. Nucis vomicæ,
Tr. Capsici, āā 3 iiss.
Tr. Gentianæ Co., ℨii.

M. Slg.—One teaspoonful in water at a dose.

These headaches, especially if there be gastric derangement, are helped by effervescing drinks. Here is a domestic prescription which is a valuable one. The juice of one-half a lemon in a pint of cold apollinaris water.

There is a form of congestive headache due to exposure to the sun, which is accompanied by dizziness, constipation and some confusion of the mental operations, and a great sense of prostration. The headache is not so intense as some others, but it is low, continuous and "muttering." With it is either an irregular fluttering, or a slow small hard pulse. There is a passive hyperæmia of the brain, notwithstanding the fact that there is pallor. Under such circumstances the improvement of the heart's action will do more for the sufferer than local remedies. Digitalis in increasing doses, its administration being guided by the behavior of the patient, ice bags to the back of the neck and diffusible stimulants, such as ammonia or alcohol are the indications. Cold douches to the head, and the application of heat to distant parts may also be required.

A congestive headache due to insolation of an active type, is often benefitted by aconite in small and repeated doses, or veratrum viride either in combination with the bromides or alone.

There is an imperfectly developed congestive headache that may occur in anæmic patients, as the result of head work.* Wood thus speaks of this form of trouble; "headache is another of those fortunate symptoms which are of a character to make themselves so felt as to force the attention of the brain

---

*Brain-work and over-work, p. 125.

worker. The head is often the seat of unpleasant sensations which are not headache, but which, as the signs of mental over-driving, are of even more serious meaning than is headache. Such are a sense of weight on the top of the head, a feeling of constriction of the forehead, or a more general cephalic distress. Such phenomena occurring after long continued strain, are very significant and should always be heeded." This form of suffering, is as a rule, associated with insomnia, lassitude, inability at concentration, great depression and irritabilility, and often by actual pain. The headache is always most aggravating after hard work, a long day in court, the preparation of a sermon, or speech, a difficult case or a sleepless night. I have met with a variety of headache in men between forty and fifty, in which profuse discharge of limpid urine, and some irregularity of heart action betoken a profound impression made upon the sympathetic nervous system. As in other headaches of the congestive type, dizziness, pulsating carotids, tinnitus muscæ volitantes and contracted pupils are often recognized.

Sub-occipital headache of a sympathetic type is also not uncommon among brain workers, and is undoubtedly due to some hyperæmia of posterior cerebral parts due to the inefficient action of the vasomotor nerves governing the vertebral arteries.

Woakes[*] describes a form of congestive occipital

---
[*] London Practitioner, 1878 p. 262.

headaches, attended by feebleness of the arms, running at the eyes and nose, blueness and coldness of hands, and at the end of an hour culminating in an attack of vomiting. Two hours after the onset of the sub-occipital pain there were superadded general pains of the back and neck and great prostration. The symptoms Woakes compares to those of mild poisoning by tobacco, but there was no vertigo. The patient had been subject to migraine for several years and was weak, sallow and emaciated. Camphor, or ice held in the mouth would cut the attack short. This author is inclined to believe this form of sub-occipital headache a sympathetic disorder, and due to reflex irritation of the gastric branches of the pneumo-gastric and to dilatation of the vertebral artery. This patient's neck was painted with a strong solution of camphor and the headache was speedily relieved.

The cutaneous nerves at the back of the head which are brought into relation with the ganglia through the medium of the plexus of the vertebral artery doubtless, when stimulated by the external application, produced contraction of the blood-vessels.

In headache due to overwork it will, of course, be suggested to every intelligent physician to regulate his patient's mode of life; to advise rest and recreation, and prescribe remedies directed to regulate the cerebral circulation, and improve the nutrition of the nervous tissue. Irregularity of intellectual work is perhaps more conducive to headache of this kind and cerebral exhaustion than anything else. The hyperæmia of the brain which is brought about by abnormal use of that organ is eventually succeeded by capillary dilatation, and a passive condition takes the place of an active one. Working under pressure, or at hours when one's fellows are abed is to be deprecated. So, too irregularity of mental habits, improper care of the stomach, and the fictitious aid of tobacco and stimulants are at the bottom of much trouble. One of the worst headaches I ever knew was in the person of an editor who ate a hearty supper, commenced his labors shortly thereafter, and at ten o'clock drank a pint of strong black coffee he nightly made in a *bigen* in his office.

Such patients need the phosphates, and are more benefited by these preparations than any other. The judicious addition of remedies which improve vascular tone, such as nux-vomica and its derivatives is counselled.

I. append a number of formulæ:

℞ Strychnine sulph., gr. i,
Cinchon. sulph, ℨ i,
Acid phosphorici dil.
Syr. limonis, āā ℥ ii

M. Sig.— ℨ i in water after eating.

This combination occasionally produces gastric trouble and I then use the following in preference:

℞ Tr. nucis vomicæ
   Glycerinæ, ää ℥ ss.
   Acid phosphorici dil.
   Syr. zingib, ää ℥ ii.

M. Sig.— ʒ i in water after eating.

In many cases there is a great deal of cardiac weakness when the habitual use of small doses of nitro-glycerine (gr. $\frac{1}{50}$) morning and night do good. For such patients I have also employed a pill which is the following:

℞ Zinci phosphidi, gr. iv,
   Ext. physostigma venenos, gr. xii,
   Ext. gentianæ, gr. xlviii.
M. Sig.—Ft massæ et divid in pillulæ No. xlviii.

Sig.—One after each meal.

This combination is indicated especially when there is a suspicion of mental trouble or impending central disease as is the following:

℞ Tr. digitalis, ℥ ss,
   Syr. hypophosphiti Co., ℥ viii.
        (Fellows'.)
M. Sig.—One to two teaspoonsful thrice daily.

The improvement of surface circulation in congestive headaches due to brain exhaustion is a prime necessity. Morning bathing in water colder than the body to which sea salt has been added, is to be advised, and I have been in the habit of using an artificial salt made by Mr. R. Fingerhut, cor. 28th st. and

4th ave., New York, which contains a large amount of potash and oxide of iron in combination. One package of this salt is to be placed in a bath-tub of warm water in which the patient is to remain ten minutes before retiring.

For the immediate relief of the headaches I rely upon cold applications and sub-occipital cupping; absolute rest and quiet. Occasionally, a large dose of the bromide of potash does good, and in those excitable cases when the hyperæmia takes place in an ordinarily anæmic brain it is especially good. Fothergill in his admirable paper in the West Riding reports has fully explained the philosophy of this form of hyperæmia, which he believes to be due to cell irritability.

The use of chloroform is very popular with English practitioners, and Day recommends it in the congestive headaches of aged people.

The following is one of his formulæ, which I have used for several years.

℞ Spts. chloroform, ℳv,
Liq. ergotæ ext., ℳxx— ʒ ss, .
Aquæ puræ, ad ℥ i.

M. Sig.—To be taken three times a day.

The congestive headaches of school children are not only due to over-work but to gastric and intestinal causes. The appearance of the child is characteristic, and abundant evidences of cutaneous suffusion are present. The headaches are throbbing, accompanied by irasciblity, and are worse after eating, or towards the latter part of the day. Bad dreams, night terrors and a clouding of brain action are accompaniments, and such children are apt to be dull at school, or uneven in their capacity. Sometimes we find them to be of the neurotic temperament so graphically described by Maudsley. They are usually bright in some things and very stupid in others. In some cases the headaches which are always aggravated by digestive disturbances and confinement in school, are the precursors of more aggravated cerebral mischief, and even of tubercular meningitis. They are best treated by anæmiants such as the bromides. A combination of the bromides is excellent, and the largest dose may be given at bedtime:

℞ Sodii bromidi,
Potass. bromidi,
Ammon. bromidi,
Calcii bomidi, ää ʒ ss.
Syr. Rubri, ℥ ij.

Sig.—One to three teaspoonsful in water, thrice daily or when needed.

Removal from school, gymnastic exercises, salt bathing and open air exercise are of the utmost importance, and it will be found that if some preparation of phosphorous is given at the same time, much good will result. I think in many cases iron is contraindicated, and it not only increases the headache, but disturbs the already impaired digestion. When it is given it should be in some assimilable form. The syrup of the iodide is the best of these, and in combination with cod-liver oil we very promptly see its good effects.

℞ Syr. Ferri iodidi, ℥ ss.
　　Ol. Morrhuæ, ℥ iiiss.
M. Sig.— ʒ ij to ℥ ss, t. i. d.

In some cases of headaches in children the use of the syrup of the bromide of nickel is recommended. It is best prepared by the combination of carbonate of nickel with dilute hydrobromic acid, and five grains should be contained in each teaspoonful of syrup. This is especially beneficial when there is much restlessness and emotional activity. Many headaches of early life are due to injudicious diet, and especially to the consumption of large quantities of meat. The influence of a preponderating nitrogenous diet has been shown to increase the number and frequency of epileptic paroxysms, and I have repeatedly witnessed its bad influence in the development, not only of disturbed sleep, but hysteria, and congestive headache.

The headaches which are so often connected with cardiac hypertrophy and renal disease, are common, especially in middle aged persons. I have already spoken of a passive variety, but there is an active form as well which is associated from time to time with conditions in which the arterial tension is suddenly increased from even slight causes. In winter, especially when the cutaneous circulation is poor, we find that these subjects are most often troubled, and attacks of head pain are common in persons who eat and drink to excess, and take little or no exercise. The possessors of such congestive headaches present facial evidence of cutaneous engorgement, amounting often to a purple suffusion, acne and dilated capillaries. The pulse is hard and full and the urine is scant and loaded with phosphates or urates. Slight exertion is followed by great fatigue, and the headaches are dull, throbbing and often preceded by drowsiness. The head pain is often attended by costiveness, and relieved by purgation. The general state of the patient must be attended to. Blue pill and colocynth are both excellent, and have a traditional reputation which has not been diminished by time, and has been handed down by our port-drinking ancestors. A capsule like the following may be given occasionally at night.

℞ Hydrarg. massæ,
   Ext. colocynthii.,
   Ext. fel. bovis., ää ℨ i.
M. Divide in capsulæ No. xv.
Sig. One or two at night.
Or,
℞ Podophyllin, gr, i.
   Hydrarg. massæ, ℨ i.
   Ext. nucis vomicæ, gr. iii.
M. Divide in pillulæ No. xii.
Sig. One at night when required.

An excellent pill for the relief of the intestinal condition, especially when the headaches are attended with drowsiness and depression of spirit is the following:

℞ Ext. nucis vom., gr. vi.
Hydrarg. chlor. mite., gr. vi.
Ext. Hyoscyamiæ,
Pulv. ferri. exissicatis.
Pulv. aloes, āā gr. xxiv.
Ft. massæ et divide in pillulæ No. xxiv.   M.
Sig.   One every other night.

Lemaire-Picquot, and Bartholow both speak highly of arsenic in congestive headache. The former was the first to suggest its use in those cases where the signs of atheromatous change were visible, and when there was drowsiness and other symptoms dependent upon loaded vessels.

The use of small, repeated doses of calomel, say one-half grain nightly, relieves hepatic congestion, and if it is followed up by Sprudel salts in the morning its efficacy will be much increased.

Some patients of this class do well on the saline waters, Hunyadi Janos, or Mattoni.

For the relief of the headaches themselves a variety of remedies have been suggested. Ergot and the bromides rank high as cerebral anæmiants. These two remedies should not be given together under any circumstances. The aqueous extract is preferable to any other form of ergot, and does not derange the digestion. An active and convenient preparation is the ergotin of Bonjean, but it is more expensive than the American aqueous extract and no more efficacious.

The combination of aconite with other remedies of this class is advisable, provided there be no decided cardiac disease, and I have used the following with success:

 ℞ Sodii bromidi.,
   Ammon. bromidi., āā ℥ ss.
   Chloral. hydratis, ℨ ii.
   Tr. aconiti rad., ℨ iss.
   Aquæ menth. pip., ad ℥ iv.
 M.
 Sig. A teaspoonful twice daily, or oftener if required.

Some congestive headaches in elderly people are probably in great part meningeal, and ergot under such circumstances is to be at once tried. Its action is prompt, and I have never seen anything worse than gastric derangement in consequence of its extended use.

In congestive meningeal headaches, and these are often exhibited by great muscular restlessness mental confusion, injection of the eyeballs, belladonna is a valuable remedy. The following prescription is worthy of an extended trial:

 ℞ Tr. Belladonnæ, ℨ ii.
   Potass. iodidi, ℨ vi.
   Aquæ anisi, ℥ iv.
 M.
 Sig. One teaspoonful in a wineglassful of Vichy water after each meal.

The doses should be increased as tolerance is established.

Dr. Wm. C. Glasgow, * of St. Louis, has called attention to a very ingenious system of treatment which is of service in congestive headaches of a familiar kind, viz: the abstraction of blood by pricking the cavernous bodies and relief of the constriction. Dr. Glasgow speaks of his experience as follows: "The disturbing cause (vascular distension) is seen in the frontal headache brow-ache, or so called catarrhal headache radiating from the root of the nose; it may be limited to the forehead; it may be felt as a dull, throbbing pain in the temples; it may give rise to intense dull ocular pain, or, extending over the head, it may be felt in the occipital region occuring frequently from cold or exposure. We also find it often conjoined with certain vaso-motor disturbances of the mucous membrane. It is frequent at the menstrual epoch, coincident with the turgescence of the cavernous bodies and is the cause of many of the so-called nervous headaches, or uterine headaches with which a similar condition of the cavernous body will be found. If we examine the nasal chamber during the attack of congestive headache, we shall find the cavernous bodies in a state of tension; they may not be greatly swollen or enlarged, but to the eye the condition of the mucous membrane is that of tension and fulness.

---

* N. Y. New Jour., Sept. 3, 1887.

The degree of tension corresponds in measure with the severity of the headache.

"A few years ago I treated those cases with hot alkaline sprays, gently applied, and the use of hot fomentations combined with the use of the usual constitutional remedies. This mode of treatment has not been altogether satisfactory and during the past four years I have substituted for it the local abstraction of blood, for which I can allege unqualified success.

* * * * * * * * * *

A simple bleeding may relieve the headache, or it may have to be repeated in a day, a week, or a month. I have seen but four cases which were not permanently relieved by a bleeding repeated from two to six times. * * * To produce the bleeding no cut is required, the cavernous body is simply pinched and the blood flows freely until the tension has been reduced; then it ceases. The amount of blood drawn rarely exceeds one ounce. In many cases it is less than this, and in many cases a single drachm of blood removed will give the required relief. In cases of extreme congestion the flow will equal several ounces before it ceases. The quantity of blood being dependent upon the distention of the vessels and this corresponds with the severity of the symptoms."

One of the most common forms of headache is that known as migraine, and two varieties are recognized with reference to the pathological states which give it origin. The form that now interests us is the *angio-paretic*. It is a clearly nervous headache, and one of a sympathetic nature. The subjects of such headache are usually those who inherit some neurotic tendency, and I have known of several generations of the same family who have been victims. Not infrequently is it associated with epilepsy, and if we go back into the family history we may find a history of phthisis, insanity or various disorders of the pulmonary or nervous systems. A large portion of the cases are women, and it seems to bear some relation to the menstrual periods, being worse with dysmenorrhœa, and often ceases, even in bad cases, with the arrival of the menopause. It is a unilateral headache affecting more often the left side of the head than the right, and is more or less sudden in its development, so far as the attack is concerned. The patient may feel a sense of malaise or languor and a chilliness and drowsiness, and shortly afterwards a smart twinge of supra-orbital pain. Others follow, and the face, which was perhaps pallid, becomes red and congested. The pain may invade one side of the head alone for a time, but eventually involves the whole head so that both sides are affected. The pain is intense when established; throbbing, burning and insupportable. The eyes are bright and suffused, the bodily temperature is sometimes elevated, and the patient is restless and excited. Darkness relieves to some extent the photophobia, and the most secluded and quiet spot is sought. Every noise intensifies the patient's sufferings, and the jar of a passing wagon, or a noisily closed door disturbs him. After a variable period of suffering, the continuity of the pain is broken or it again becomes paroxysmal, or muttering, like the thunder at the end of a storm. At this time nausea may occur, and the patient more or less successfully empties his stomach. It is a mistake to suppose that this symptom indicates that the didestive organs are necessarily at fault. Though such headaches have been called "sick headaches" they are not as a matter of course due to the condition of the stomach, and it is probable that this symptom originates from an irritation of the pneumogastric. The headaches often bear no relation to the state of digestion—they come after or before a meal or when digestion is most perfect. There is a tendency in migraine to chronicity, and attacks may occur daily. The pathological state is an unequal paresis of the muscular fibres of the vessel coats and the repeated attacks lead to a varicose condition, and possibly to miliary aneurisms.

In the treatment of this form of congestive headache two indications present themselves: 1. The improvement of the general system. 2. The relief of the attack itself. The migrainous patient is often an anæmic individual, and the anæmia is of that kind which is the most troublesome. There is often a disposition to make fat, and a tax upon the nervous system, which directs the function of the sympathetic nervous system into other directions. There is a vast amount of useless tissue that demands blood that is needed elsewhere and the balance of vascular tension is constantly interrupted—one moment the brain is anæmic, the next congested. The cerebral vasomotor nerves lose their tonus and a condition of unequal angio-paresis occurs. Such patients need iron and digitalis, tri-nitrine or strophanthus.

In the relief of the headaches themselves we may resort to diffusible stimulants, and I have for many years resorted to the treatment, which consists in the administration of large and repeated doses of the muriate of ammonia—20-grain powders should be prepared and these should be given in a large quantity of water every hour until the headache is broken up. Some patients are relieved by repeated large draughts of green tea, or black coffee. Effervescing draughts of bromo-caffeine act in much the same way.

Bearing in mind the irritability of the brain in such cases and the existence of the headaches as a relation to epilepsy – it may be well to resort to the bromides. The use of this class of drugs should be continuous and without relation to the actual occurrence of attacks. Large doses may be given thrice daily, and do more good than their irregular administration; or, if the attacks are periodical, with reference to the time of the seizures. Chloral hydrate may be combined with the bromides but care must be taken not to form the habits of *chloralism*.

℞ Sodii bromidi, ℨ iss.
   Chloral. hydratis, ℨ vi.
   Aquæ anisi, ℨ iv.
M. Sig.—One teaspoonful in water morning and night.

The vascular tonus should be improved, and arsenic either in combination with strychnine or quinia is apt to help the patient and destroy the migrainous habit. This is Routh's * formula which is also excellent in malarial headaches.

℞ Quinia disulph., ℨ ss.
   Acidi Arseniosi, gr. i.
   Acidi nitrici dil., ℨ i.
   Aquæ puræ, ad ℨ i.
M. Sig.—Gtts xxx in a wineglassful of water after eating.

Elderly women at the time of the menopause are often affected with a peculiar congestive headache which seems to be connected in some way with the "flashes," which are so often the subject of complaint. The pain is often vertical and throbbing, and in some individuals is attended by very great depression of spirits.

Such headaches are relieved by agents which quiet pelvic irritability. Warm douches repeated twice or thrice daily are of benefit, and I have been in the habit of administering large doses of dilute hydrobromic acid or Fothergill's solution, which is made by the addition of tartaric acid to a solution of bromide

---

* Day on Headaches.

of potash. This should be well diluted, and from half an ounce to an ounce is sometimes required to bring relief. The use of the mustard foot bath, brisk exercise and massage are often necessary as adjuvants. These headaches are often helped by the compound spirits of ether.

Sexual excitement of a protracted kind without gratification, or what Fox calls "mental onanism," is apt to result in a variety of headache of a sympathetic nature and with all the evidences of congestion. The head pain is short lived, closely follows the cause, and is easily relieved by rest and quiet, and a large dose of any one of the bromides. I have often met with this variety in patients suffering from incipient insanity of the masturbatic type. Such young people are apt to present rather lively emotional excitement, and to be boastful and conceited at times. The pain is frontal, and accompanied by a sense of supraorbital pressure.

Spinal douches consisting either of a jet of cold water or sponging tend to arouse the dormant viscera and equalize the distribution of blood. Warm foot baths are of course excellent auxiliaries to other remedies in the acute attack. Turkish and Russian baths though admirable remedial agents are dangerous and should be used with the greatest caution. I have known of several deaths as a result of their injudicious use, and if there is the least suspicion of atheromatous degeneration or cardiac disease they should be forbidden.

As to mineral baths and water, there is much to be said which is, however, found in special works upon baleonology. The Canadian and American springs best suited for the treatment of cerebral congestion, notably the passive variety, are those at St. Leon near Quebec; Caledonia near Ottawa; St. Catherines; Richfield; Sharon and Saratoga in New York State; Buffalo Lithia Springs, Virginia; the Berkeley Springs, and the Red Sulphur Springs, Va.; Spring Lake Well, Ottawa Co., Mich.; the Wisconsin Springs (Waukesha, etc.). The foreign springs which are especially serviceable are: Vals and Vichy, (Grande Grille) France; Salzbrun, Freiburg, Hombourg, Carlsbad, Aix la Chapelle, Baden Baden; Friedrichshall, Kissengen, Marienbad, Seidlitz and Adelheidsquelle, Germany, and Leamington and Cheltenham in England. There are many others, but this list I think is sufficient.

In congestive headache, especially passive, do I advise the use of saline purgative waters and baths. It is better to give some of the stronger German or Hungarian waters than to allow the patient to *flush* himself with the milder aperients—Congress water and the like, and those which should be used in great moderation. The waters of Carlsbad or its evaporated salt, which is now for sale, while not so good as Hunyadi or Rubinat, are excellent alteratives. Pullna water heated or cold is especially beneficial in those headaches where there is much venous turgesence of the face.

The constant use of baths and douches of well regulated temperature is all important. A cold bath of brief duration for the purpose of stimulating the surface capillaries is a prime necessity. Better than the immersion of the whole body is the use of the douche or needle bath. In the absence of elaborate apparatus we may employ the ordinary "rose spray" and a rubber tube fitted to the cold water cock. Fig. 1 is an elaborate needle bath made by John Simmons, 110 Centre St., New York, which is perhaps better suited to hospitals than private houses. At a small expense, however, a practicable needle bath may be constructed and its therapeutical advantages will fully warrant a moderate outlay.

The diet of the patient who suffers from these headaches should be simple, and as a rule, consist of a reduced quantity of the hydro-carbons. It is a mistake to err in going to the extreme of entirely abolishing, as is too often the custom, certain articles which are not positively injurious. It should be our aim to reduce the labor of the digestive organs, and, therefore, it is better to give small quantities of well digested food frequently, than large quantities at long intervals. Lean meat, poultry, game, fish, eggs, the green vegetables, and stale bread, agree with persons subject to congestive headache, as a rule, better than articles of diet containing much starch or fat. Veal and pork and the watery or aromatic vegetables are to be dispensed with, as are all substance which are

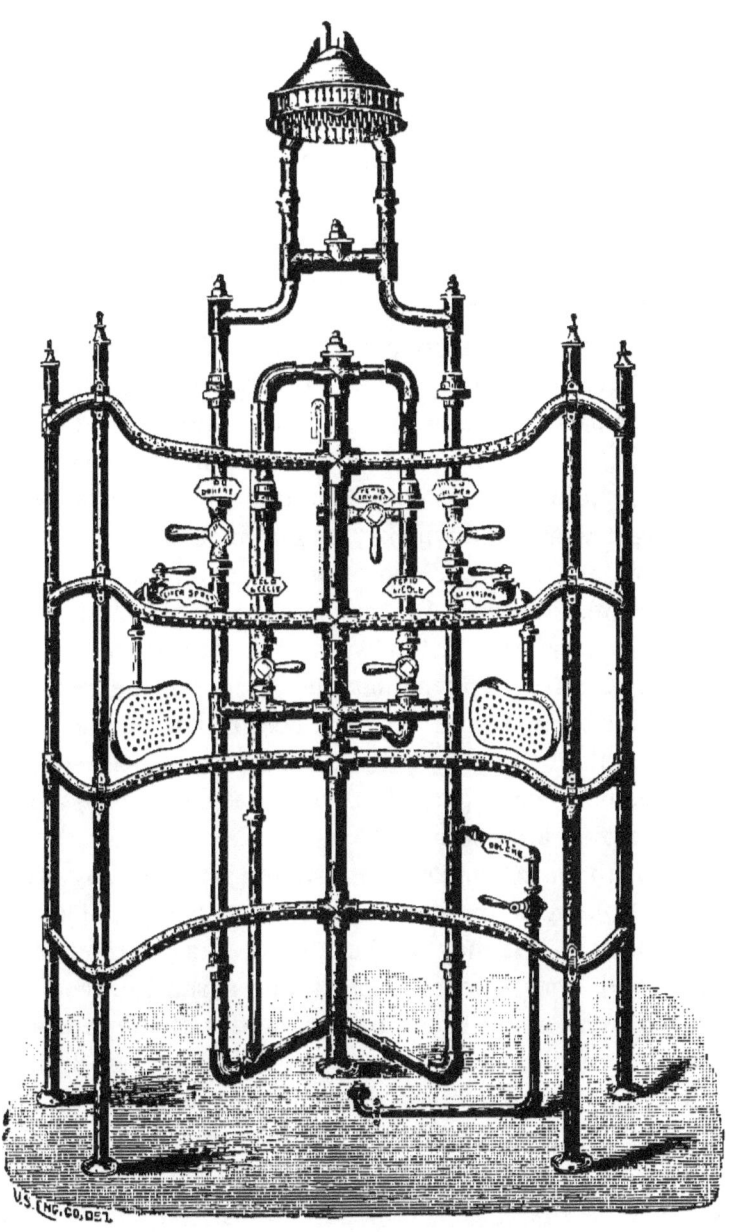

Fig. 1. Apparatus for Needle Bath.

slow of digestion. Tea and coffee are not as harmful articles as they are generally supposed to be, though of course in some instances they must be rigorously excluded.

Alcohol in some cases of congestive headache is absolutely necessary, though of course in others it is directly contraindicated. The passive hyperæmic headaches are certainly benefitted, and if the stimulant selected is a proper one, I can see every reason why it should be allowed. Brandy, Rum, Burgundy, Champagne, Port and Sherry wine, malt beverages and the liqueurs, are harmful under all circumstances, but light wines and whiskey or gin in regulated quantities, in angio-paretic conditions do much to improve the vascular tonus. In the headaches of middle or old age, they are nearly always of great service.

There are many palliatives which may be resorted to for the external relief of congestive headaches. Cold applied to the nucha, or to the top of the head by means of ice-bags; cold douches and ether spray to the temples are useful.

Benham in an excellent article (West Riding Reports, vol. iv, p. 152,) refers to the mechanism of cold as follows: " It may be that the decreased temperature and consequent lessened nerve sensibility produced by the cold upon the extremities of the sensory nerves, are shared in somewhat by the centres under the cranium, from which they spring; and thus it may be that that portion of the sensorium to which the irritation on the nerve peripheries in the stomach or elsewhere—causing headache—is conveyed, shares in the diminished sensibility of those centres, and is therefore less capable of receiving impressions as vividly as before; the sensation of pain felt by the patient being consequently much lessened. When we consider the proximity of the central tracts of the fifth, and the pneumogastric branch of the eighth pairs of nerves, it seems probable that cold applied to those peripheries of the fifth distributed over the forehead should produce such an effect in parts in close proximity to the origin of the pneumogastric as to be capable of somewhat modifying the impression in the course of its transmission to the sensorium from the peripheries of that nerve irritated by a disordered stomach." It should be born in mind that in some cases of congestive headache the headaches are increased instead of benefitted by a too extensive application or a too intense degree of cold.

I have been in the habit lately of using pressure by means of compressed sponges. These may be had of most apothecaries and are about one-half inch thick when dried. One sponge is to be applied over either temple, and both are held in place by a bandage passed several times around the head and firmly fastened. When this is secured, water may be applied, and when the sponges expand, steady and even pressure is made upon the temporal vessels. Many congestive headaches are simply due to hyperæmia of the scalp, and this limitation of blood supply is often followed by prompt relief of the pain. The use of carotid pressure by Corning's method also produces temporary relief, and in certain frontal headaches firm pressure applied on the root of the nose is an immediate palliative.

External stimulating or irritant liniments do little or no good and only produce redness or vesication, except when the headache is of the kind just mentioned. Menthol applied in the form of cones sometimes relieves the head pain, but it is a temporary and uncertain remedy at best employed in this way. An alcoholic or etherial solution used with the atomizer is far preferable.

Bearing in mind the physiological operation that follows the irritation of the cervical sympathetic or the upper part of the cord, recourse may be had sometimes to the actual cautery or blister for the purpose of effecting local revulsive action of a sharp and limited nature.

The well-known action of the galvanic current upon the sympathetic nervous system suggests its use in congestive states of the cerebrum. The cathode may be placed on the superior cervical ganglion of the cervical sympathetic, and the anode on the forehead. Very mild currents from two or three cells are sufficient, and under all circumstances the operation should be conducted with great care. Electrical irritation of the sympathetic ganglia is known to produce contraction of involuntary muscular fibre, and the rationale of its effects in cerebral hyperæmia will be apparent. The application should last but a minute or two. It may also be made by means of large sponge — or cotton — covered electrodes one being placed upon the top of the head and the other at the back of the neck. Sub-occipital headaches are decidedly relieved in this way.

Faradism is of benefit in headaches which are due to congestion of the scalp, or when the object sought is the relief of internal pain by the reflex irritation of cutaneous filaments. Great care should be taken not to interrupt the galvanic current, and I would urgently recommend the use of the water or wire rheostat.

The improvement of the surroundings of the sufferer from habitual headaches is a part of the duty of the careful practitioner, for there are many patients whose trouble does not yield to medicines but is constantly aggravated by local causes. Many a congestive headache is due to bad heating and ventilation. Furnace heat, weather strips, and windows rarely opened in winter, together with bad plumbing, are responsible for much misery. Injudiciously selected clothing, sedentary habits, and irregular hours contribute their share, and often the individual selects a dwelling place which is entirely unsuited to his state of health. A low altitude, where the temperature and barometric pressure are not high, agrees with most of the victims of cerebral congestion, or headaches due to such a pathological condition; and mountainous districts are to be avoided as places of prolonged residence.

CHAPTER II.

ANÆMIC HEADACHES.

Cerebral anæmia is far more common among women than men, and in a very large number of instances is a feature of the depressed condition of the nervous system dependent upon loss of blood, and uterine disorder. In others, it is due to loss of blood from hemorrhoidal fluxes, general malnutrition, and debilitating causes of many kinds. It is confined to no age, but is usually most pronounced in women during the catamenial years.

The anæmic headache is rarely continuous, though in some individuals, it exists in a dull unpronounced form with occasional exacerbations of decided pain. It is accompained by a sense of very great vertical pressure and throbbing. At times it is associated with neuralgia of the fifth nerve. The patient is pallid, has enlarged pupils, a small weak pulse, pale lips and buccal mucous membrane. The tongue is apt to be indented, furred and pale. Digestion is weak, and palpitation common. An aortic murmur is often heard, the sphygmographic tracing is almost straight; and the number of red corpuscles is greatly reduced.

Cold clammy hands and feet, phosphatic or limpid urine, great muscular fatigue, and insomnia are characteristic. In many individuals there is decided tenderness of the spinous processes and the *vertebra prominens* is especially tender.

In some women these headaches occur with great mental depression just after the menstrual period, and this is especially the case where there is menorrhagia. They often recur daily, and in patients under treatment, where iron is given, and the uterine condition not improved, it will be found that just before the menstrual period, and when some recuperation has taken place, that there is a marked diminution in the character and severity of the attacks, with subsequent relapse however.

The anæmic headache is more pronounced in the early part of the day. In fact the patient commonly awakens with some nausea and head distress. This may often be abated by a cup of hot strong tea, or ammonia in some form.

Fothergill, in writing of anæmic headache, says in one of his early contributions: "The pain is dull, persistent and unvarying, and the sensation is not uncommonly as if the skull was opening, or the upper half of the calvarium was being lifted off. Chronic headache in conditions of cerebral anæmia is usually, or at least often, vertical; while frontal headache is rather associated with passing conditions of exhaustion from sustained intellectual labor. The why of this will be seen presently.

Vertical headache is most distinctly associated with anæmic conditions of asthenic gouty states, and is often of much diagnostic value, often, also, pointing very clearly the direction which our therapeutic measures must take if we wish them to be successful. At other times headache, often vertical, sometimes frontal, is found along with those anæmic states when the patient complains chiefly of "low spirits," simple states of mental depression and unhappiness, from a defective blood supply to the encephalon."

The bromides and chloral are useless and aggravating remedies in such forms of headache and should never be given. In some cases of anæmic headache when the seizure is unilateral, in fact when we have an angino-spastic migraine, the use of bromide is indicated, but only then. I much prefer cannabis indica which may be given in pill form in increasing doses, commencing with one-eighth of a grain of the extract, and increasing until mild toxic effects are reached. When such headaches occur about the menstrual period a mixture of the bromide and cannabis indica is an excellent one.

  ℞ Ammon. bromidi, ℥ i.
    Tr. cannabis ind., ℨ vi,
    Mucilag. acaciæ, ℥ iv,
    Ess. menth. pip., ℨ ii.
  M. Sig.—One teaspoonful thrice daily in water.

The bromide of ammonium seems to exercise a special influence on the uterine functions, and in cases of disturbed sympathetic regulation and ovarian pain, which are common accompaniments, the relief afforded by the above combination is very considerable.

Sometimes it is admirable to combine the cannabis indica with a hyperemiant. I have found the following useful:

    ℞   Ext. cannabis indicæ, gr. vi,
           Ferri ammon. citras, gr. xlviii.
    Ft massæ et divid in pillulæ No. xxiv.
    M. Sig.—One thrice daily.

It is of the greatest importance that the disturbance that leads to the uterine hemorrhage should be found and remedied. In cases of simple relaxation, when there is no organic difficulty, the use of gallic acid, or hot syringing has done good in many cases. In some of my patients a lacerated cervix, intra-uterine polypi, or fibrous tumors have been at the root of their anæmic headaches.

I have lately seen a number of cases of anæmic headache where the cause was found to be the loss of blood from some unsuspected source. Two or three of these had hemorrhages from the rectum as the result of hemorrhoids; one had attacks of expistaxis; and I discovered the cause of an almost constant headache in a person who had lived in the tropics, to be hæmaturia which was the result of malarial disturbances and filaria. A lady sent to me by Dr. D. Bryson Delavan, of this city, had vertical anæmic headaches of great severity, and bodily exhaustion which was at times alarming, and in this case there existed hæmophilia. Bleeding from the gums, nose, dysenteric fluxes and menorrhagia, or rather metrorrhagia were the causes of the drain. It is always well in these cases to inquire as to the existence of such possible troubles and remove them by appropriate means. In the case of hemorrhoids of course there is nothing effective but surgical procedures. In the other cases our reliance must be upon astringent remedies and hæmiants. Gallic acid alone, or with the acetate of lead, astringent injections of various kinds, and iron or arsenic are to be made use of. Those who have described or seen much of such diseases as progressive pernicious anæmia, or other conditions in which the red corpuscles disappear, find that arsenic is often superior to iron—a conclusion with which I am inclined to agree. Such idiopathic disorders as those of which I speak are undoubtedly neurotic, and the value of arsenic is a matter of easy, practical determination. When iron does good in such cases I have found the alkaline or neutral preparations better borne and assimilated than the others. The older French writers placed great reliance upon the carbonate, the peroxide and the mild salts generally, and the Germans have given us the malate, which is an easily digested and excellent preparation. The albuminate,* or peptonate, may be selected when there

---

* In the N. Y. Médical Record, Aug. 28, 1884, I first called attention to the value of the albuminate of iron in anæmic and hysterical women, and those with idiosyncrasies

is much of the gastric feebleness which is pronounced in so many bloodless women. I have combined the albuminate of iron with the carbonate of soda *in small quantities*. We must not lose sight of the fact that the use of soda in large amounts, or of Vichy water, is quite apt to hamper our efforts at cure by blood impoverishment, and other alkaline mineral waters should be forbidden as well.

With manganese as a substitute for iron, I have had little or no experience, and such as I. have had is not encouraging.

During the past few months I have found that the appropriation and conversion of iron in the system is helped by the conjoint administration of some substance rich in oxygen. Oxygen gas itself has been

who often declare their unwillingness or inability to continue the iron even in most minute doses.

In 1871 Diehl announced the discovery of the albuminate of iron, which after all is not a true salt.

Miahle has held that "the albuminate of the peroxide of iron is formed in the blood, and that this is the basis of the red globules," and it has been shown that the presence of an alkali favors the catalytic change. Some iron salts are absolutely inert as remedies, and pass unaltered from the body. Among these are the ferro and ferricyanides of potassium, and other double salts which are not precipitated by the alkalies. The combination of iron and albumen with an alkali seems to be at once a measnre likely to be of value from a therapeutic point of view, and so I have found it. The preparation I use is in lozenge form, each containing about twelve grains of the albuminate of iron.

used for this purpose for several years by many French therapeutists and by Dr. A. H. Smith and others in this country, and I have used nitrous oxide gas. If the permanganate of potassium be given alternately with any soluble preparation of iron it will immeasurably increase the good effects of the latter, and if the former be made up with coca butter it will produce no gastric irritability or intolerance. Five grains of the albuminate or ten grains of the sub-carbonate may be taken after eating, and one-half to one grain of the permanganate in a tablet before eating.

Fothergill advises the combination of arsenic, sulphate of iron, nepaul pepper, and the pills of aloes and myrrh.

In the headaches due to imperfect cerebral circulation and heart weakness, I place much reliance upon strychnia and drugs of its class. The following is an excellent tonic:

    ℞ Strych. sulph., gr. ss.
        Ferri et quin. citras, ℈ivss.
        Digitalis pulv., gr. xxiv.
        Ext. hyoscyamiæ, gr. xlviii.

M. Ft. massæ et divid. in pill, no. xlviii. Sig.—One after each meal, to be increased.

Digitaline which has been recommended by many, is, I am convinced, a dangerous and unreliable remedy, and occasionally produces collapse, or obstinate vomiting. I prefer the older preparations provided they be fresh. In cases of chronic cerebral anæmia with lowered arterial tension I have used strophanthus, which is safe and not cumulative. In some recent cases I have obtained aid from the following:

℞ Bruciæ, gr. i.
　Tr. ferri chlor., ʒ vi.
　Infus. digitalis, ʒ iv.
M. Sig.—One teaspoonful in water after each meal.

When the anæmic headaches are attended by varied symptoms of general nervousness, and fall under the head of "neurasthenic," we find much benefit from the phosphates and hypophosphites. Day recommends the combination of the hypophosphite of soda with a bitter tonic. In combination with one of the cinchona series, provided the dose of the latter be not too large it is excellent. Quinia though physiologically indicated, often aggravates an anæmic headache when administered in unsuitable quantities. The anæmic brain is irritable, and as I have before said is liable to hyperæmias of rapid development.

A congestion is likely to occur from a dose of quinine that in the ordinary individual would scarcely be appreciated, and the anæmic headache may be replaced by another of a different type. I therefore make use of *very small doses* of the sulphate of quinine or cinchona, or sometimes prescribe Huxhams' tincture. Some of us wonder why many of the proprietary combinations of iron, quinine and strychnia either do no good, or else aggravate the patient's sufferings, but it is not surprising that an arbitrary proportion of component parts will not suit every case. The physician should use his own judgment more often than he does in dosage. "Ready mixed" medicines are apt to be convenient to the busy man, but unreliable.

In cases of anæmic headache with depression, the administration of opium in combination with iron and phosphorus, is likely to do good, but on no account should the patient be told what remedy is given him.

℞ Phosphori, gr. i,
Opii pulv., gr. xx,
Ext. belladonnæ, gr. v,
Ferri redacti, ℈iv.

Ft massæ et divid in pillulæ No. xl.
M. Sig.—One morning and night.

For the relief of the same complication we may order cocaine in combination with dilute phosphoric acid and quinine.

℞ Cocaini hydrochloratis, gr. vi to viii,
Quininæ sulph., ʒ i,
Tr. ferri chlor., ʒ v,
Acidi phosphorici dil., ʒ i,
Syr. aurantii flor., ℥ iv.

M. Sig.—One teaspoonful thrice daily in water.

When there is constipation, a state very common in cerebral anæmia, and attendant mental depression; it is important to clear the lower bowel, and aloes or its derivative aloin is indicated.

The following will do for occasional use:

℞ Strych. sulph., gr. i,
Ext. belladonnæ, gr. viii,
Aloin, gr. xii,
Ext. fel. bovis ʒ iii.
Divid in capsulæ, No. lx.
M. Sig.—One or two every other night or when needed.

Saline purgatives are not suited to anæmic patients, nor are alteratives such as iodine or its compounds, with the exception of the iodide of iron.

In cases where there is much insomnia and depression, opium may be given with some mixed cathartic, and Day's formula is a good one:

℞ Ext. opii
Pulv. rhei, āā gr. i,
Pil colocynth co., gr. iss.
M. Sig.—At a dose at night.

I have found paraldehyde to be well borne and free from disagreeable after-effects. It is best given in capsules and each soluble capsule should contain ten minims. ♏ 30—♏ 60, repeated if necessary, will usually secure sleep. It does not seem to have any analgesic effect.*

The elixir of absinthe is an excellent menstruum in the tonic prescription. I have used it as well as the

---

*In large doses it is sometimes excreted in great part by the axillary sweat glands and, as the odor is far from sweet, the result is often embarrassing to the patient.

elixir chartreuse, and am sure it has helped many anæmic women, with headache due to depleted brains, and both are of service when there is an antipathy which is often purely notional, against wine.

℞ Ferri. iodidi., gr. xxxii.
    Tr. stramonii, ʒ iii.
    Elixir absinthii., ℥ ii.
    Syrups simplicis, ad. ℥ iv.
M.
Sig.—One to two teaspoonsful in water after meals.

℞ Ferri. et potass. tartras., ʒ vi.
    Aquæ bull., q. s. to dissolve.
    Tr. belladonnæ, ʒ iiss.
    Elixir chartreuse viridi., ad ℥ xii.
Sig.—One to two teaspoonsful every four hours in water.

℞ Ferri. et cinchonidiæ citras., ℈ iss.
    Fl. Ext. gossypii. radicii. corticis., ℥ i.
    Elixir chartreuse viridi., ℥ iv.
    Aquæ anisi., ℥ viii.
M.
Sig.—One to two teaspoonsful in water every four hours.

The above is of benefit when the anæmic headaches are due to some uterine drain and relaxed muscular fibre.

Diseases or defects in the apparatus of respiration and which interfere with the proper oxygenation of the blood are quite apt to induce anæmia and chlorosis, which may lie at the foundation of headaches of a constant and distressing nature. Any obstruction of the upper air passages is prone to interfere with the free admission of air to the lungs; and this difficulty may consist in the enlargement of the tonsils, or depend upon various diseases of the nasal fossa. Hypertrophied turbinated bones and polypi have been found by Curtis and others to account for persistent headaches among their patients, and the use of the nasal trephine has worked wonders in cases that have resisted drugs. I have myself cured many headaches by the removal or reduction of enlarged tonsils in children, and in two cases epileptic paroxysms have ceased to recur after this operation. If the patient is disinclined to permit surgical measures, it will be found that the careful application of chromic acid will cause a cicatricial reduction of the glands.

In some asthmatic individuals or sufferers from chronic capillary bronchitis or emphysema, such headaches are by no means an uncommon result of defective oxygenation. Belladonna or its alkaloid may be made use of with confidence, for they act well in most cases.

Aged people of spare build and gouty habit are apt to suffer from anæmic headaches, the explanation of which is probably gouty spasm of the vessels, and a limited anæmia. The headaches are often accompanied by insomnia, and by weakened digestion. In such cases much can be done with the diffusible stimulants, and Hoffman's anodyne agrees well when given alone, or with ammonia. The moderate use of alcohol by such patients is in every way advantageous, and I prefer for them either a good rye or Scotch whiskey taken at meals, or a very dry champagne. Horseback or tricycle exercise is to be counselled, especially when the person is performing intellectual labor. Many such persons live upon farinaceous, and so-called health foods of a cereal nature, which under the circumstances are about as injurious as can be imagined. Oatmeal is no exception and its use should be forbidden. Fats are also bad.

The general treatment of these persons should be supporting. Phosphorous is contraindicated but not arsenic. The use of soda in combination with the bitter tonics is apt to do good in improving the weak digestion that usually accompanies the condition and the old formula so familiar to most practitioners of the bicarbonate of soda and tincture of gentian, and the syrup of rhubarb with perhaps a few grains of the carbonate of ammonia will often prove to be of great services.

There is an alarming form of headaches which anæmic children sometimes present, and the apprehension consists in the fact that it is symptomatic of a grave disorder which is ultimatively fatal. I allude to the formation of the hydrencephaloid condition of Marshall Hall; or the deposition of adventitious substance in the brain. Distention of the perivascular spaces characterizes one of these, and the pressure of a tuberculous mass may produce anæmia, both of which result in severe and constant headache. If vomiting be present with such head pain, and the child becomes listleness and stupid, a very grave outlook may be taken. Decided and prompt alterative measures are imperative. Cod-liver oil, phosphorous, feeding, and possibly the iodide of potassium with belladonna are indicated, and if the child be at school it should promptly be removed and sent into the country.

Sinkler * has called attention to the occurrence of migraine which he believes is more common among children than is generally suppposed. His conclusion that it may begin at the eighth or ninth year, must be accepted by those who see much of children's headaches. He goes further by stating that the form of the disease being thus early, is apt to disappear at full development (i. e. adult life). I cannot agree with him in this so far as girls are concerned.

Sinkler insists upon the use of fatty food—cod-liver oil, cream or butter—the exhibition of bromide in small quantities, the correction of possibly existing ocular defects, and "in all cases of migraine we should look carefully into the condition of the teeth, and have unsound ones filled or removed."

Two new remedies have been suggested for the cure of headaches—antipyrine and acetanilid, or antifebrine.

In January, 1887, Ungar related his experience with antipyrine in the treatment of hemicrania, and in

---

* Medical News, Oct. 29, 1887.

March Dr. C. B. Lyman, who had been induced to try the remedy after the publication of Ungar's success, administered it in several cases of neuralgia of the cervical, facial, and supra-orbital or mixed varieties, with more or less benefit. The first of these observers experimented with it as a successor to the salicylates, which had proved to be of great value in his hands in several varieties of headache, and he witnessed no evil results from doses of even 23 grains. Lyman used an initial dose of 15 grains, repeated two or three times if necessary, and relieved the paroxysms, but did not prevent their recurrence. In March last* I began a trial of this drug, and afterward its successor, antifebrine, in a variety of headaches, in insomnia, and in epilepsy. Some of these cases had been treated with more or less success with the salicylate of sodium, and the usual remedies, and the cases of epilepsy were under modified bromide or other treatment. The cases of headache selected were those of migraine of the angeio-spastic and angeioparetic varieties, as well as ordinary facial or sub-occipital neuralgias; and the cases of epilepsy which were chosen were those of the symptomatic form complicated with objective and subjective indications of cerebral disease, as well as the simpler forms which seemed to be dependent upon continued states of cerebral ischæmia, cerebral instability, etc.

In angeio-spastic migraine with evidences of

---

* N. Y. Med. Jour., May 28, 1887.

cutaneous anæmia, dilated pupils, and coldness, the headache commencing in the morning, I found that both antipyrine and antifebrine would quickly abort the paroxysms after the first dose.

Miss. T. had taken salicylate of sodium in doses of gr. xxx repeated once or twice, with variable relief. Cannabis indica and the chloride of ammonium failed to do good. Her headaches were connected with sexual irritation and excitement. She was very anæmic and hysterical. One powder of fifteen grains of antipyrine relieved the pain in less than an hour. The repetition of a daily dose in the morning completely suspended the headaches for a period of two weeks during which the patient was under observation. She was put upon a course of iron, which she took meanwhile.

Mrs. R. suffered from vague headaches, a sense of vertical pressure, and general anæmia which was largely due to frequent uterine hemorrhages. After the catamenia, and during the first half of the month she had attacks of angeio-spastic migraine. Five grains of antifebrine produced tinnitus, but relieved the headache. This patient subsequently obtained slight relief from cannabis indica.

I have used these drugs in a large number of cases and have given as much as 45 grains of the antipyrine in two hours, a comparatively short space of time. Antifebrine is the safest, and though one case is reported where large quantities produced a variety of disagreeable symptoms, I can only say from my own experience that I have never seen anything but temporary unpleasant consequences. Antipyrin may be administered hypodermically in doses of eight or ten grains in an equal quantity of water. Sée,[1] who has used it, believes it to be superior to morphine, and it has none of the disadvantages of the latter. Of the local analgesic properties when used in this way I will say more when we come to the discussion of neuralgia.

Dujardin-Beaumetz recommends ethroxy-caffeine, a new drug, but it should be used with the greatest caution for it is dangerous and unreliable.

 ℞ Ethroxycaffeine, gr. xii,
  Sodii salicylat, gr. xv,
  Aquæ destill., ℥ iiss,

Sig.—From five to ten teaspoonsful as indicated.

Of other comparatiuely untried new preparations of this series, I will not speak.

Iodoform is an excellent remedy in some cases of intractable anæmic headache in strumous subjects and may be given in repeated doses alone, or with iron.

The citrate of caffeine is of value in anæmic headaches, but should be given in much larger doses than are generally prescribed—it rarely has much effect in less than five grain doses. Various effervescing salts such as the "bromo-caffeine" or the effervescing citrate of caffeine taken when the

---

[1] Les Nouveaux Remédes, Dec. 8, 1886.

headache first appears will often arrest it. I have obtained good results from a distillate of coffee made by Mr. Angelo, of this city, at my suggestion, and use it in half dram and dram doses, well diluted.

I have lately used salol—another coal tar product—in several cases with good effect. The dose is five grains, to be repeated. Antipyrine is quite soluble in water, but antifebrine sparingly so.

Germain Sée recommends that these drugs be given in ice water which counteracts their depressing effects on the digestive organs.

Betol or naphthalol, which was introduced by Neushe of Bern, is useful not only in anæmic headaches but those of a neuralgic character.

Moxon recommends morphine in headaches with extreme prostration and sickness, when the extremities are cold and the pulse is feeble and the patient has been days without getting relief. In such cases one-sixth grain of morphine with the addition of $\frac{1}{80}$ grain of atropine are injected hypodermically at regular intervals.

Some years ago, at the suggestion of Dr. John E. Blake, I administered nitrous oxide to anæmic patients as an hypnotic, and incidentally found that its value was very great when anæmic headaches existed. The ordinary apparatus used by dentists was that tried, and I turned the valve so that air was admitted in varying proportions. I have within the past ten years used the nitrous oxide treatment in hundreds of cases—many being those in which headache was a feature. My conclusions as I have elsewhere said are that not only is the assimilation of iron very much increased when gas is administered but the integrity of the cerebral capillaries is brought to a much higher standard. The clinical results are the improvement in sleep, a gain in weight and color; and the subsidence of headache. The gas should not be given to the point of insensibility—or great vertigo— but as soon as any tingling of the lips or tongue is produced, its use should be discontinued for a few minutes. Four gallons of mixed gas and air should be given daily.

Certain drugs which rapidly congest the cerebral blood vessels are of service. Among these as immediate remedial agents I may mention nitrite of amyl (which by the way is not an entirely safe remedy), and trinitrine or nitro-glycerin. The first named may be used at the commencement of an attack, or inhaled in small quantities several times daily. The latter may be given in tablet form or in liquid combination with iron.

The patient should be made to seek a recumbent posture so that the head shall be to some degree lower than the rest of the body, and he should lie in this way several hours daily.

The diet of all patients with headache of anæmic origin should be of the most nutritious kind and largely nitrogenous. As the digestion is weak the food should be selected with great care, and given frequently. Milk peptonized or skimmed, the beef peptonoids. Koumyss (that with the true Russian ferment the Cranmoor being the best), or Matzoon which are easily digested milk preparations; butter-milk which is serviceable in the gouty cases; eggs, beef juice or raw meat should form the staple diet, while articles which simply satisfy hunger or stimulate the appetite should be given only when the patient has recovered his power of assimilation. The good effects of condensed food are most conspicuous when enforced rest is obtained. The so-called "rest treatment," is often a misnomer. It may be so purely an arbitrary and ill-suited therapeutical measure as to do more harm than good. Not only is the patient's bad physical condition aggravated, but many a woman is made hypochondriacal or worse. The term has covered a multitude of blunders. Like everything extreme, it is powerful for good or evil, and should never be resorted to, except with a due consideration of the patient's exact state, and what is to be accomplished. It does not do to put any or every woman to bed, as has been the fashon of past years, for no two cases can be managed in exactly the same way, and one woman will grow nervous and more miserable under the compulsory "rest" that may cure' another. The real end in view should be the prescription of rest that will prevent the expenditure of nervous force in muscular movements, from exceeding the production of energy and food assimilation. Nothing more or less. This means watchfulness and care, a good nurse, sometimes removal from home when the patient is unreasonable, hysterical or fanciful; regularity in eating, passive movements and massage when needed, skin stimulation by spongings of dilute alcohol; or faradization when the woman tires easily. One of the greatest benefits of massage is the exercise it affords, without the use of volition, and when the effort of volition is tiresome, the tone of the muscle is improved by the exercise effected by another.

General faradization by means of broad sponge-covered electrodes, and mild currents passed generally over the body are beneficial. In persons with weak digestion, galvanization of the sympathetic is advantageous.

In many cases anæmic headaches are connected with gastric derangements which need treatmeut. Bismuth, the bitter tonics—calumbo being the easiest of digestion—quassia and the peptonoids should be used as occasion requires. The capacity of some women to make blood is so poor that nothing can be done for their headaches until their digestive power and assimilation are strengthened, and it does little good to give iron or specific drugs while no gain is being made in other directions.

In very extreme cases—the method of rectal injections of fresh blood—dried blood, or beef juice made in suppositories with gelatin may be necessary. These headaches often exist in women who have hysterical vomiting, when besides moral treatment some such means as those just suggested are in order.

The mineral springs, which best suit the subjects of chronic anæmic headaches, are of course those of a chalybeate nature. The Rockbridge alum and Sweet Springs of Virginia, Columbian Spring of Saratoga and Sharon are all within reach in this country; and those at Bournemouth, Tunbridge and Hastings Wells of England, Spa of Belgium, St. Moritz, Switzerland, Schwalbach, Pyrmont, Alexis-Brunnen are the best known in Europe.

Most of the foreign and domestic iron waters as well as the arsenuiretted waters are bottled and may be had without trouble.

CHAPTER III.

ORGANIC HEADACHES.

Nothnagel,* one of the most practical of all German writers, is not disposed to attach much importance to the significance of headache as a diagnostic sign in organic brain disease; he even goes so far as to say that in chronic cerebral anæmia he doubts if headache is actually due to the chlorosis (sic.) or the anæmia itself, for the intense and pernicious anæmia which is produced by carcinoma is rarely expressed by headache. It cannot be denied, however, that the constant existence of localized pain, or of pain associated with other symptoms, is suggestive of mischief within the cranium, which is more or less grave, and is to be taken out of the category of functional disorders. The location of a constant pain often points to cerebral abscess, and this is especially true when this lesion is a result of aural disease.

The most familiar form of headache of the kind of which I speak, is that associated with syphilis in some of its stages. When we find a nocturnal headache of very great intensity, it is usually of specific origin.

"There is no description of headache," writes Dowse, "and one might say, no kind of pain, which

---

*Wiener Med. Presse, No. 13, 1879,

equals in intensity that which results from a localized hyperplasia of the dura mater."*

It is sometimes almost unbearable, and varies in character. In cases where the bones of the skull are involved it is diffused, and affects the entire scalp, is deep and increased by contact, and in this respect somewhat resembles rheumatismal headache. The headaches of syphilis are also of a localized character, and may in this respect resemble clavus. In old cases the pain seems to disappear when the cerebral mass is invaded, and the dura is not subjected to so much pressure as in the beginning. It is not usually connected with tibial pain. When it is a feature of syphilitic epilepsy it, as a rule, precedes the paroxysm. In the early stages of the disease it may be of a light character and both nocturnal and diurnal. Some authors speak of a headache of a low grade with paroxysms of great severity, and exacerbations which occur every few weeks as the result of depressing causes. Dowse describes this form very graphically: "The pain is of a different kind to that of the other forms of headache; it is of a dull heavy aching character. It has no central point from which it radiates. It is usually diffused more or less over the whole of the forehead, and gives to the patient a hang-dog look; often the complaint is that the eyelids cannot be raised, they feel so heavy; the whole of the vessels of one eyeball

---

*Syphilis of the Brain and Spinal Cord, Part I, p. 24. London, 1879.

may be congested and not the other, or both may be similarly affected." Temporary ptosis, squinting diplopia, vomiting, tinnitus, somnolence, slow speech, monoplegiæ, and a variety of greater or less troubles suggest syphilis. I have always been suspicious of headaches with attendant stuporous symptoms or vertigo.

Our therapeutical indications are simple, and one can hardly go wrong, for the list of efficient drugs is so small. My reliance is upon the iodide of potassium, *but in large doses.** I have cases under treatment at present who are taking one hundred and twenty grains thrice daily, or more than half an ounce in the twenty-four hours, and this quantity alone keeps the disease in check and the headaches absent. In most cases it is safe to begin with ten grains, three times daily, in water. A saturated solution is better dispensed than any other, and more convenient, and the daily dose can be at first increased one drop, then two, then five, until the point of tolerance is reached. It does no good to give large doses when coryza is produced and saturation indicated, but the patient should be kept on the border line. The iodide is best given in alkaline solution, and I prefer Vichy water as a vehicle. If this plan is followed the patient will not be

---

* Taylor says: "A fraction of a grain of corrosive sublimate, or three to five grains of the potassium iodide, administered three times a day, will do no more good than would the water in which they are dissolved." P. 663.

annoyed by the unpleasant metallic taste or gastric derangement. In persons who cannot tolerate iodide this way, I have followed the advice of my friend, Dr. Keyes, and administered it in milk. In some cases mixed treatment may be employed after a course of the iodide.

A pill of great service in anæmic cases of cerebral syphilis is the following:

℞   Pill hydrarg. massæ,
     Ferri sulph. excissicat.,
     Ext. hyoscyamiæ, āā gr. xlviii.
M.   Ft. massæ it divide in pillulæ No. xxiv.
Sig. One thrice daily.

This combination is especially good in the early headache of the disorder.

In these cases, and those more advanced, we may hasten improvement by inunctions, either of the old-fashioned blue ointment, or of the 20-per-cent. oleate of mercury; mercurial baths are sometimes excellent. Both ergot and opium give the patient much relief, and particularly the latter. I have lately use antipyrine and antifebrine with good effect. Much comfort is derived in these and other headaches from the use of cold applications to the head, and a convenient and cleanly apparatus is the head-coil, made of India rubber pipe. One end is attached to a vessel filled with ice water, the other hangs over the side of the bed and discharges into a suitable vessel. An effectual method of cooling the head was devised by Hughes, of St. Louis, who applies sulphuric ether to the scalp. For immediate use there is nothing better than the ice bag filled with ice and salt, and changed from time to time.

The headache of meningitis either pachy, or lepto, is, as a rule, diffused and very intense. That of the first named is ordinarily chronic, may be of traumatic origin and is dull and connected with suffusion of the face, redness of the conjunctivæ, and is accompanied by some of the symptoms of cerebral congestion. The characteristic pulse which was described by Nothnagel is sometimes irregular, and when there is irritation of the pneumo-gastric nerve in basilar cases there is periodical acceleration. Confusion of ideas, mental weakness and feebleness of memory are often present, and when there is a meningo-encephalitis we are quite apt to have cortical sclerosis, delusions of grandeur and dementia. The headache in chronic cases is always present, but just as in the form of syphilis just mentioned, there may be painful exacerbations of an acute character, which are neither confined to day or night, but are precipitated by exposure to the sun or by excitement.

Belladonna, ergot and opium are the three remedies which promise most in the way of relief, and these should be used energetically. The first may be give to the toxic point, and the second in doses as large as can be borne by the stomach. Less than one-half dram of the fluid extract thrice daily does little or no good. The belladonna in combination with the potassium iodide is an excellent form of continuous treatment. Small doses of the bichloride of mercury act nicely sometimes even when there is no suspicious of specific disease. In cases of rheumatismal origin the salicylate of soda in good full doses repeated frequently in alternation with the acetum opii will often lull the pain. Aconite and gelsemium are recommended. The latter is spoken of very highly by Bartholow, especially when there is a febrile state, where he recommends ♏v. doses of the fluid extract repeated every two hours, so as to maintain a uniform physiological effect. The extreme method advised by the Germans, which consists in shaving the hair and painting the scalp with croton oil, is not believed to do much good, nor is extensive cauterization or blistering.

Cerebral tumor is a fruitful cause of organic headache, and in an excellent article in Pepper's System, the statistics collected by the writer show that of 100 cases of cerebral tumor 66 patients complained of headache, which was described as "torturing," or agonizing in twenty instances.

The headache of cerebral tumor is very intense, and has been looked upon by many clinicians as one of the chief indications and before the days of absolute (?) localization as of pathognomonic importance. The pain always bears more or less relation with the situation of the growth. With tumors of the convexity it is situated anteriorly or posteriorly or laterally, when we may find motorial or sensorial symptoms upon the other side of the body. In one case alluded to by Rosenthal "the headache was accompanied by painful sensations and formications in the right arm; these symptoms disappeared after a time and were replaced by an anæsthesia of the limb. At the autopsy, a tuberculous tumor of the size of a walnut was found upon the convexity of the left cerebral hemisphere; the pathological changes extended to the deeper portions of the brain, lesions of which are accompanied by anæsthesia of the limbs." Of five cases of gliomatous tumor three complained of no pain whatever. These authors find that cerebellar tumors were not necessarily associated with occipital pain.

A headache of intense character with monoplegias or more extended losses of power, convulsions or vomiting, is always suggestive of an adventitious deposit; and if the symptoms are irregular, the patient having great pain which subsides after a comparatively long siege and return again with a new accession of motorial or sensorial symptoms, the diagnosis is strengthened. This temporary disturbance may be and often is suggestive of an accomodation of the brain to the pressure.

Organic cerebral headaches are as a rule preceded by symptoms of greater or less significance and are not of sudden onset. Such headaches as a rule are intractable and puzzling. Headaches due to tumors are often mistaken for those of a functional nature, the existence of the growth being unsuspected. I can recall two cases where a profound central anæmia with headaches of a commonplace type existed for a long time, and only after death were large central growths found. Happily the ophthalmoscope will usually reveal the existence of neuritis and choked disk. The symptom of a suspected central change may turn out after all to be the manifestations of a general condition and Wood relates a case of headache of this nature in his excellent work.

The patient was a man who suffered for years from agonizing headaches of daily occurrence. In time the headaches became associated with petit mal- and Wood made the diagnosis of organic disease of the brain. At last the small joint and some of the larger ones were attacked simultaneously with a furious sudden and general gout, with deposits, etc., etc., when the headaches were relieved to some extent. The patient was entirely crippled but had his headaches only occasionally. Wood was led to believe that this was originally a gouty thickening of the dura mater with deposit.

Percussion of the skull is a useful diagnostic means in determining the location of a tumor at the convexity, but care should be taken not to confuse scalp tenderness with that of a more subtle nature.

The therapeutical indications are varied. In the case of tumor we are to diminish the pressure caused by the presence of the growth, and lessen its irritant effects. One of the peremptory hygienic measures which is applicable in this form of organic trouble as well as others, is the abstinence from anything that may increase the cerebral blood supply. Mental labor, alcoholic indulgence, heated rooms, and over-eating, are all apt to aggravate the pain. The hair should be kept cropped short and the head gear should be light and well ventilated. Tight collars should be discarded. The use of cups to the back of the neck, occasional bleeding, such as has been recommended by Dr. Glasgow, and leeching the nostrils, or scarification will afford the patient relief. Of course cold applications are in order.

So far as medicines are concerned one may empirically use the potassium or ammonium iodide, both in large doses. Hypodermic injections of morphine atropia or antipyrine are to be resorted to when the pain is intense, and the mixed bromides are useful. The combination of the iodide and bromides is a good one in nearly all forms of grave cerebral disease:

 ℞ Potass. iodide, ℨ v.
   Sodii bromidi, ℨ iss.
   Potass carbonas, ℨ iij.
   Tr. columbo, ℨ viij.
 M. Sig. One teaspoonful thrice daily.

Galvanism and faradism should be given a trial and the former especially will often relieve an organic headache, though of course only temporarily.

Now that cerebral localization has been of such great aid to the surgeon, and "brain surgery" has become a measure which is not necessarily a very dangerous one so far as operations that do not result in opening the dura mater are concerned, it seems as if relief might be afforded more often than it is; especially when evidence of cortical pressure are concerned; and when there is evident tension of the most tolerant of the meninges.

CHAPTER IV.

TOXÆMIC HEADACHES.

Under this head may be included the form of head pains which are due to the retention in the blood of various substances which may be the production of disease, or the result of administration, unconscious or otherwise. Among the first I may mention lithæmic headaches, uræmic headaches, the headaches of fever, of drugs, of tea and coffee and tobacco, and of metallic poisoning. Though pathologically some of these might better be described under the head of congestive or anæmic headache, I think their clinical characteristics prominent enough to entitle them to separate description.

An experience of many years has taught me that lithæmic poisoning is at the bottom of many functional nervous diseases, as well as some organic ones. Its effects are shown in a multitude of perversions of sensibility, and even motility, and the importance of toxæmia due to retained nitrogenous substances is too often unrecognized or disregarded.

Many individuals of the gouty habit, without actual classical gout, but with a thousand and one erratic symptoms, are the subjects of headaches which readily disappear when a proper alteration of habits and food is made and when they are placed upon remedies of a suitable nature. The subjects of such headaches are often men, and more usually those past middle life, though the headache of lithæmia is confined to no particular age. The victims are usually of sedentary habits, whose powers of excretion are impaired, and who meanwhile live upon articles of food which are improperly assimilated. Editors, literary men generally, lawyers, doctors, clergymen, clerks and others who are compelled to spend long hours indoors, and who rarely use their voluntary muscles are quite subject to attacks of head pain, and such states mark the accumulation of uric acid. The urine is loaded with the familiar brick-dust sediment; it is scant, and often is passed frequently, and they have an annoying tickling or burning sensation in the urethra. The bowels are constipated, digestion is slow and poor and there is flatulence. Sleep is broken and bad, and disturbed by dreams and eructations of wind. The patient is depressed, morbid, easily fatigued; has muscular soreness, and formication, perhaps, of his finger tips, feet, tongue, lips or buccal mucus membrane. Mental work or physical exercise is irksome and disagreeable, and he has diffused headache and heaviness over the orbits. There may be frontal pain, and it may be worse on arising, or may take a migrainous type and be very sharp and distressing. In some cases there may be some alteration or complication of remote joint pain of the ordinary gouty type. If the urine be examined, it will be found to contain the oxalate of lime and the lithates. When the specific gravity of the urine is lowered and when the bowels become regular, the passages losing their clayey color and consistency which belongs to them; there is some amelioration of the headache. These headaches are often attended by giddiness and tinnitus and by gastric derangement.

Haig,* who has devoted much attention to the relation of headache to the excretion of uric acid conducted a series of observations: "Meat and cheese were taken with the object of bringing on a headache, for purposes of experiment. The relation of this headache to the excretion of uric acid at first appeared equivocal, but definite results were obtained on separating the urine excreted during the headache from that before and after. There appears to be retention of uric acid before the headache, excessive excretion during the headache, and diminished excretion after the headache. The excess during, balances the diminution before and after; there is no absolute excess of uric acid; hence the previous equivocal results. During a headache there is little or no alteration of the excretion of urea. The theory which best explains everything in this connection is that of diminished alkalescence of the blood. A dose of acid, either introduced from without or formed internally, may cause temporary retention of uric acid, and so lead to headache. Beer will do this. Retention pos-

---

* London Lancet, May 28, 1887; also Practitioner.

sibly does not explain everything, as the excess during headache appears to exceed the previous retention."

Both Haig and Hutchinson recognize a condition which they call "quiet gout," where there are no violent symptoms of the real disease. These patients, besides presenting the symptoms I have above detailed, present as well the indications of hereditary influence, and what Hutchinson speaks of as the "irritable hyperæsthetic and tired eye." The treatment of such headaches must consist in the reformation of habits, both of eating and drinking, and the indulgence in exercise of a proper sort.

Meat is to be partially, if not altogether, dispensed with; and cheese and other highly nitrogenous substances discarded. No wine or beer should be allowed, and the green vegetables, fish, oysters and poultry are to form the staple diet.

The exercise provided for the patient should be that taken in the open air, but when this is impossible, I would suggest the use of Ruebsam's or other rubber gymnastic apparatus, the "rowing machine," dumb bells, or Indian clubs. An hour in the gymnasium has cured the headache of many a hard-worked clerk, and tennis, football, baseball, or other good out-door sports where there is general muscular exercise, are of importance.

The salicylate of soda, iodide or acetate of potash, the preparations of mercury or colchicum are useful, and suited to different cases and conditions.

Haig uses the former in small doses, two or three grains being given every quarter of an hour for three or four doses. I believe that larger doses are of greater service, and I rarely give less than ten or fifteen grains, and direct the patient to take the salt continuously for several days. It should be well diluted and always taken when the stomach is not entirely empty. In some cases it may be combined with success with iron when there is anæmia, but there are few methods of doing this for the two agents do not readily combine. Peabody* has devised the following formula which is compatible:

 ℞ Acidi Salicylici, gr. xx.
   Ferri pyrophosphatis, gr. v.
   Sodii phosphatis, gr. j.
   Aquæ, ℥ ss.
 M.

He gives this dose which is a rather large one every two hours. It may with propriety be diminished in the cases of which I speak.

 Dr. J. Solis Cohen,† of Philadelphia, has furnished another combination which is perhaps more agreeable:

 ℞ Sodii salicylatis, ʒ iv.
   Glycerini, fl ℥ ij.
   Ol. gaultheriæ, ♏xx.

---

*Medical News, Dec. 11, 1886.
†Medical and Surgical Reporter, May 28, 1887.

Tr. ferri chloridi, fl ℨ iv.
Acidi citrici, gr. x.
Liq. ammonii citratis (B. P.), q. s. ℥ iv.
M. Sig. ℨ ij in water three or four times daily.

When salicylic acid or its compounds produce dizziness or gastric distress, the dose should be diminished.

Salol in doses of from five to ten grains acts sometimes much better than the salicylates.

In some cases the headaches will only succumb to colchicum which may be administered in combination with alkalies:

℞ Vini sem colchici, ℥ ss.
Potass. acetas,
Potass. iodidi,
Tr. cimicifugæ rac, ää ℨ v.
Aquæ menth. pip., ℥ iv.
M. Sig. One teaspoonful every four hours.

Some of the older combinations of colchicum and opium are energetic and will often promptly break up an attack, for example:

℞ Ext. colchici acetici, gr. xxiv.
Ext. opii, aq., gr. vi.
Ext. colocynth co., gr. xviij.
M Ft. massæ et divid in pill. No xxiv.
Sig: One or two every four hours when pain is acute.

The use of small doses of calomel during the continuance of the lithæmic state is likely to result not only in an improvement in the function of the liver, but correspondingly in the cerebral circulation.

In headaches due to pure cholæmia, when there is much drowsiness, and sometimes a light degree of mental aberration, the use of the above pill, or of large doses of phosphate of soda will relive the apathetic condition of the organ. In this form of cephalalgia which is, as a rule, diffused, the mineral acids and strychnia are also indicated, and acid baths and general cutaneous frictions are likely to be followed by greater elimination of bile. All such patients should seek a high altitude and dry climate, and should indulge freely in exercise of all kinds.

Uræmic, or rather renal headaches are familiar forms of troubles. They are not distinctive so far as location is concerned, though many of them are basal and posterior, with ocular pain and frontal and vertical pressure. The conjoint symptoms of disease of the kidneys, urinary and otherwise, makes the diagnosis clear, and the head pain is apt to keep pace with or be modified by the condition and amount of the urine. Attacks of headaches are likely to follow a sudden diminution in the amount of urine voided, though this is by no means the invariable rule. Vomiting, a tendency to somnolence, and some alalia are indications of a rather desperate state of affairs, and in such cases the headache is likely to be followed by coma. The constancy of the dull pain, and the presence of conspicuous nervous symptoms, are sometimes likely to suggest the existence of cerebro-spinal meningitis, and the prolonged manifestation of light grades of speech and psychical disturbances, with profound sub-occipital pain tends to lead even the most careful diagnostician into the commission of an error. A case of this kind came under my care sometime ago, which had been pronounced meningitis by one of the ablest clinicians of the city, and I accepted his opinion almost without question. The patient's somnolence deepened almost into coma and there were suspicious forebodings of convulsions. Her urine became scant, and when examined abundant evidences of waxy kidney were found.

A prompt recourse to hot air baths, diaphoretics and remedies directed to favor elimination resulted in an immediate lightening up of symptoms and an eventual disappearance of the headaches. They then returned some time afterwards when the patient became careless in her habits, and after two or three months of suffering she died.

Wood speaks of the headaches which may occur in the pre-albuminuric stage of gouty kidney when the vessels are rigid and the arterial tension raised. This headache, however, cannot be said to be fully due to retained effete material. It is hardly necessary to remind my readers that meat should be excluded from the bill of fare, and stimulants of all kinds rigidly tabooed. A light nutritious, farinaceous and vegetable diet, with milk, or a milk diet alone, is that most likely to agree with the patient. Agents which increase the action of the organs of excretion should be vigorously employed. In many cases the uræmic poisoning is associated with anæmia of a profound type when we may resort to iron—and the old-fashioned muriated tincture is the best. This may either be given with digitalis, or strophanthus; or these agents may be tried alone. In some cases the use of tri-nitrine is attended with the happiest results, and convallarin which is a perfectly safe remedy may be prescribed when digitalis is likely to produce gastric irritability.

The compound jalap powder at night, or any of the purgative mineral waters do good when an extensive process of renal degeneration has taken place.

In some cases acetate of potash either in combination with digitalis or nux vomica will mildly stimulate the kidneys and increase cardiac tonicity. Nux vomica is I am convinced a better remedy in many cases than digitalis and when our desire is to coax the kidneys we may use with propriety.

℞ Tr. nux vomicæ, ʒ iii,
Potass acetatis, ʒ i,
Infus. digitalis, ʒ viii.

M.—One to two teaspoonsful, every three hours or oftener.

A good reliable pill for many years in use at the old New York Hospital is the following, and is especially valuable when the disease has led to anasarca.

℞ Pulv. digitalis
   Hydrarg massæ
   Pulv. scillæ, ää gr. xlviii.
M. Sig:—One every night or oftener.
Ft massæ et divid in pillulæ No. xlviii.

These have a mild diaphoretic as well as diuretic action.

Malarial headaches which are so common in many parts of this country are really of a congestive type. They are not always distinctive and the term is too often made use of when a definition must be given, and the medical man is not exactly sure of what he has to treat. The headache can only be recognized with certainty when it has a periodical character, and disappears with the use of quinine, and other anti-periodics. Though the pain may be associated with fever and sweating, the chill being absent, it is a rare condition of affairs, and we now often find headaches of this kind which are the direct results of an impoverished condition of the blood; a sequel rather than a part of the malarial attacks. The pain is often suboccipital, and when it is periodical, it is frontal, very intense, commening in or over one eyeball. It is commonly confused with supra orbital neuralgia, but is probably a hyperæmia of one hemisphere, a species of angio-paretic migraine. It is attended by great misery and suffering and a paroxysm rarely subsides under several hours. Sometimes it alternates with the chill. Quinine in very large doses, the other salts of cinchona, Warburg's tincture or the expissated extract, and arsenic are all useful. In many cases the hepatic and gastric derangement which attends the headaches must be attended to, and calomel or blue mass in combination with capsicum or ipecac in small doses is advised. If arsenic be given it should be pressed so that the appearance of slight puffing beneath the eyes, and a warning epigastric tenderness are produced. The paroxysms of headache should be treated just as the ordinary ague. With a very large dose or series of doses of quinine a few hours before their expected appearance. In one case lately seen, fifteen grains of antipyrine quickly broke up the headache, and I was not obliged to give a second dose.

As most of these patients are anæmic and debilitated, iron is naturally indicated. The tincture of the chloride is the best of these in combination with quinine. The arsenite of iron, or the water of the Rocegno spring of the Tyrol which is now imported, are worthy of a trial.

Diabetic headaches are usually the precursors of more marked nervous symptoms, and especially coma. They are diffused and connected with dizziness, and more familiar indications of the disease. They are by no means as common as the neuralgia of the lower branch of the fifth nerve which is sometimes found, or of the sciatic. A diet which excludes starch and sugar, and the use of a carbonic acid water which contains the carbonate of lithia and arsenic are the chief indications. The bromide of arsenic has been recommended.

Tobacco, tea and coffee, or narcotic drugs may produce headache of anæmic or hyperæmic character. In most cases the diminution of the amount used, or its abolition is enough to effect a cure. The headaches due to the injudicious use of the former are apt to be connected with more or less gastric disturbance, heart irregularity, fleeting pains about the cardiac region or back, coldness of hands, indisposition and muscular feebleness, and a feeling of distension with "tightness of the scalp." The pain is dull and attended with some "burning" of the eyelids, and there may occasionally be a sense of vertical pressure and light vertigo. Attacks of slight tinnitus are occasionally described. I know of no remedy which is so nearly an antidote to the bad effects of tobacco, and so quickly removes the headache as nux vomica, or its alkaloids.

The headaches which result from immoderate coffee drinking have been called by Wood *caffeinic*. My own impression and experience is that the headaches of both tea and coffee are after all due to gastric derangement with consequent malnutrition and anæmia, and not strictly toxæmic. Any one familiar with dispensary practice recognizes at once the existence of a digestive disturbance, which is probably a low grade of gastritis, and which prevails among servants who drink large quantities of tea. This is usually helped by abstinence, and diet; and the headaches cured by quinine and iron. It cannot be disputed that some neurotic persons cannot touch coffee or tea; and that insomnia, headache and a host of light nervous troubles result from persistent indulgence,

The consideration of headaches of various febrile states, and of a temporary nature more properly belongs to works upon general medicine.

CHAPTER V.

NEURALGIC HEADACHES.

A neuralgia of the fifth nerve is apt to be manifested by paroxysmal as well as dull pain, and by limited or general expression. No age is exempt, and men and women suffer alike. Its causes are various, and its duration and severity variable. If we consult any anatomical chart we may appreciate, how obscure is its origin in certain cases, especially those where the neural disturbance is due to some central change. In such instances, if the lesion be sufficiently profound, we may find not only pain, but disturbance of trophic function, and of the sense of taste in the anterior half of the tongue; as well as various anomalies in the functions of the parotid, lachrymal, and submaxillary glands.

As the results of peripheral trouble; cicatricial and otherwise; anæmia or congestion of the nerve trunk; the pressure of bony or other tumors; reflex irritation from bad teeth; and a number of other pathological changes; we are furnished with a painful affection of the nerve which has been called *trigeminal* or *facial* neuralgia, and ophthalmic or supraorbital, infraorbital, dental and occipital neuralgia with reference to the branches of the nerves that are involved. The pain is essentially paroxysmal, very agonizing when once established, and sudden in its onset. The paroxyms in a well-established attack are so closely connected as to give the impression of continuous pain. The attacks of neuralgia in a chronic case, though occasional in the beginning, tend to become more and more constant, and are readily lighted up by any exciting cause, such as a cold draught, the act of eating very hot or cold substances, fatigue or pressure. The pain commonly begins in the supra-orbital branch of the trigeminus, and when developed, involves the entire side of the head, and when acute and general, we find lightning pains which affect this region, the back of the head as well, and the teeth of both jaws.

At certain *points* where the nerve branches become superficial, we find great tenderness. These are known as *supra-orbital, palpebral, nasal, ocular* and *trochelar; infra-orbital, malar, superior labial; temporal, inferior dental, lingual, inferior labial, parietal, occipital*, and vary as one of the three or all the divisions of the nerve are affected. During the course of a neuralgia, or afterwards, we find these *painful spots*.

The neuralgic pain which involves the ophthalmic branch is a common and easily distinguished form. The pain runs over the side of the head, the nose and eye of the affected side, and is relieved somewhat by pressure over the supra-orbital foramen. The face may be flushed or pale, and the eye is bathed in tears, and there is hyperæmia of the conjunctiva. In some cases there is a copious flow from the lachrymal

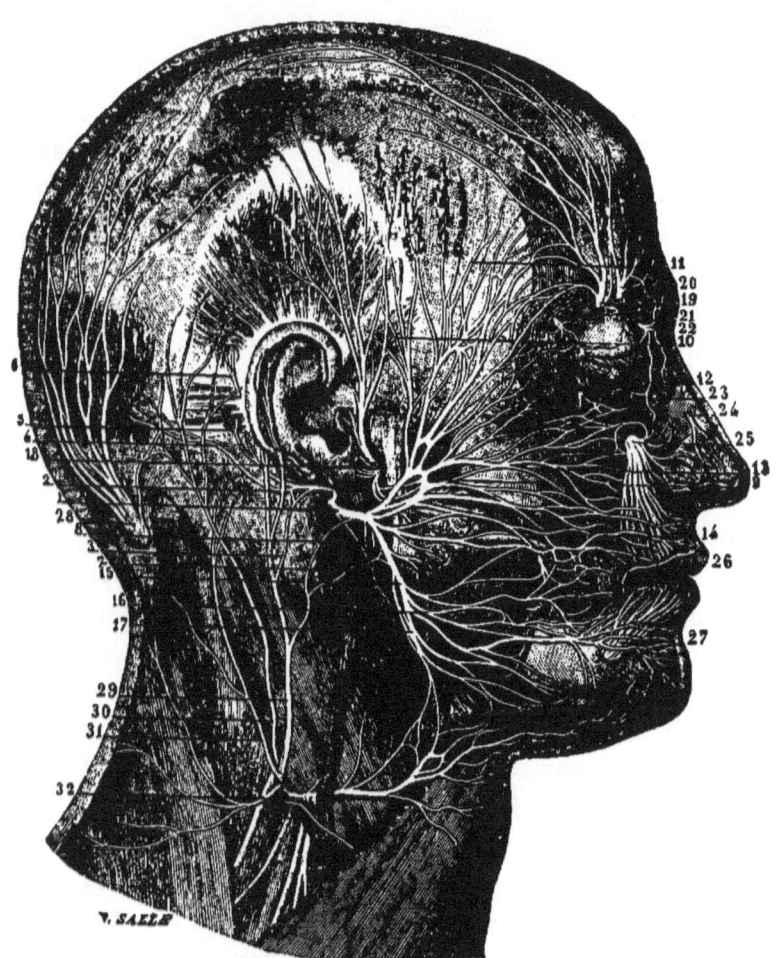

FIG. 3.
SUPERFICIAL DISTRIBUTION OF FIFTH AND SEVENTH
NERVES (HIRSCHFELD).

1. Trunk of Seventh Nerve
2. Posterior Auricular Branch of
3. Filament of Great Auricular.
4. Twig to Occipitalis
5. " Post Auricular N,
6. " Sup. " "
7. Branch of Diagastric "
8. " to Stylo-hyoid
9. Superior Division of Pes anserinus
10. Temporal Branches
11. Frontal "
12. Orbital "
13. Nasal "
14. Buccal "
15. Inferior Division of
16. Labial
17. Cervical
18. N. Temporo-Auricular
19. Supra-orbital
20. Internal Frontal
21. Palperal Twigs of Lachrymal
22. Intra-Trochlear
23. Malar Branch of Orbito-Malar
24. Ext. Nasal Twig of Ethmoidal
25. Infra-Orbital
26. Buccal Branch of 5th
27. Labial and Mental Branches of 5th
28.
29.
30. } Cervical Nerves.
31.
32.

ducts of the affected side, or the contact of air with the filiaments which supply the interior of the nose may result in sneezing, or, more rarely, a puffing up of the mucous membrane with obstruction. There is a painful point above the eye—over the supra-orbital notch. Sometimes, as in the case of Anstie, the eyebrows or hair become the seat of a change of color, and dryness, brittleness or exfoliation are the consequences of repeated and persistent attacks. Ross speaks of neuro-paralytic ophthalmia. In old cases of neuralgia we not only find trophic disorders such as I mention, but sometimes ulceration of the cornea, and persistent changes in color, consisting of pigment deposition in the skin.

The anatomical distribution of the nerve will enable us to trace the variety and character of the pain which symptomatizes neuralgia of the lower branches. Besides the painful points enumerated, we will find violent faceache and toothache which is more or less general. Sometimes the upper and lower rows of teeth on one side will be affected, or in one jaw alone. The mucous membrane of the mouth is exceedingly tender, perhaps tumefied, and in some cases a crop of herpes is present as the sign of an unusual attack. The tongue may be swollen. This, however, is rare, but it is common to find a tenderness of the gums, and sometimes a great increase in the amount of saliva secreted.

The intra-cranial causes of neuralgia are very

obscure. Vulpian reports a case of violent nature due to the perforation of the gasserian ganglion. (See plate.) Tumors, meningeal thickening, or the formation of syphilitic or other adventitious deposits, may

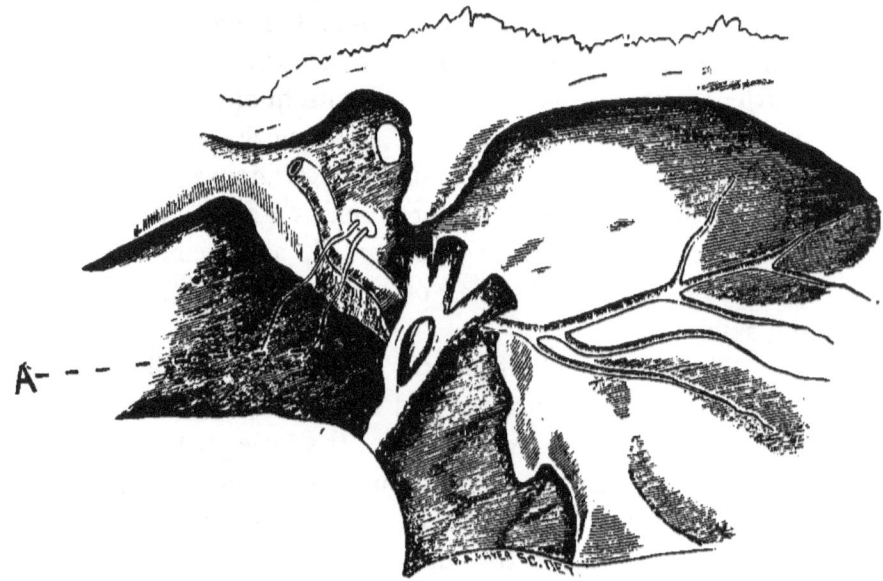

FIG. 4.

VULPIAN'S CASE.

A.—Bony spicula penetrating Gasserian ganglion.

give rise to the affection, but it is a curious fact that a syphilitic deposit may completely surround a nerve without any impairment of function.

Disease of the antrum or alveolar processes which is entirely unsuspected may give rise to severe neuralgic disturbances. A gentleman from the West consulted me who was the victim of intolerable dental neuralgia with painful shooting pains in the roof of the mouth, gums and pharynx. The slightest pressure upon any of the teeth of the upper jaw on the left side would inaugurate a paroxysm of neuralgic pain, which would finally involve the whole nerve. Soft food could be taken only in small quantities, and it was necessary to avoid extreme temperatures, for a mouthful of ice-water would cause intense neuralgic twinges. Two molars had been drawn without relief, and all methods of treatment were made use of unsuccessfully. Upon his return home a dentist extracted one of his bicuspids, which contained a verylong root, and this was removed with great difficulty. A profuse discharge of pus followed and after a few days the pain disappeared and never returned.

The simpler cases of neuralgia due to cold (especially the ophthalmic form) malaria or gastric trouble, are relieved by anodynes, and the local use of galvanism. I have already spoken of the malarial headache which is often neuralgic, and have specified the antiperiodic remedies. It remains now for me to refer to the virtues of certain drugs which seem to have a decidedly specific action upon the trigeminus. The most important of these is aconite or its alkaloid aconitine. The tincture of the root may be used, in large doses, so that decided toxic efforts are produced; carefully feeling the way. Small doses are almost useless. Perhaps the most convenient form of the drug is its alkaloid. Duquesnel's aconitia is the best, and the dose should vary from $\frac{1}{300}$th to $\frac{1}{60}$th of of a grain, to be repeated. A sufficient quantity to help the disease will produce some prickling of the tongue and lips, shivering, and a feeling of subjective coldness; and may even produce numbness of the extremities. The pulse should be watched and the dose regulated with reference to the heart's force. It is unwise to give aconitia in pill form, or in a manner that may interfere with its solubility, and the danger of a cumulative dose is great. I have used it for years either in tablets (the Fuller method) or in solution.

The plan of using aconitine adopted by Dr. Séguin and by him suggested to the N. Y. Therapeutical Society is the following:

 ℞ Aconitinæ (Duquesnel's), gr. 1-10 to 1-6.
   Glycerinii,
   Spts. vini rec., ää ℥ j.
   Aquæ menth pip., ad ℥ ij.

 M. Dose, ℥ j t. i. d. before eating, to be carefully increased.

Another remedy of value is the croton-chloral hydrate which also has a direct action on the fifth nerve. In doses of from fifteen to thirty grains, it is given in water and will occasionally modify the pain.

The salicylate of soda, antipyrine or acetanilide have been spoken of before in connection with other forms of headache. They are all useful in neuralgia. Wilks recommends chloride of ammonium in fifteen grain doses, three or four times daily, but I believe this does good only in a limited number of cases, and these are not examples of true neuralgia, but migraine.

Tonga, a Fiji remedy of great local reputation, has been extensively employed in England and America. It is of unquestioned value in some cases of supra orbital neuralgia, and may be administered in the form of a fluid extract, and in doses of from one to two teaspoonsful, to be repeated.

Cimicifuga, in combination with aconite and belladonna, has been recommended by Metcalfe in sciatica. I have also used the combination in facial neuralgia with success. Equal parts of the tincture of cimicifuga racemosa or actea racemosa, tincture aconite root, and tincture belladonna are to be combined, and doses of six drops are to be repeated every hour until relief or physiological effects are produced.

Ammoniated copper has been praised by the French writers. I have never found it reliable and hesitate to recommend it.

The treatment of the general condition which leads to the development of neuralgia is important. Arsenic, iron, cinchona and its alkaloids; alteratives such as mercury and the iodides, the phosphate of silver, and many others makes a formidable list. I have, in speaking of anæmic headaches, given some formulæ, and here have nothing more to add except it be to reiterate the advice that the exhibition of all drugs of a restorative nature should be in large doses. The silver salts are indicated in inveterate cases, and I prefer the tribasic-phosphate of silver to any other —even the nitrate. It should be given with argillaceous earth, for the confection of roses, and other vegetable excipients are very apt to decompose the silver salts which are exceedingly unstable.

Some chronic cases are materially benefitted by Donovan's solution an old and valuable combination, and others by the use of one of the iodides of mercury, preferably the red. The salicylate of iron may be suggested in cases of gouty origin.

In sub-occipital neuralgia, which is commonly of malarial origin I place great reliance upon large doses of quinine carried to the point of cinchonism.

In cases of facial neuralgia with zona ophthalmica or herpes, there is no better remedy than that I have just mentioned, in addition to galvanism. In fact the indications are those which lead us to select the same treatment in herpes zoster.

Phosphorous in its pure form is one of the best regenerators of diseased nerves in existence, and in neuralgia of the fifth nerve is an excellent agent. The solution in absolute alcohol which I believe was first recommended by Thompson, of England, is an admirable preparation and produces little or no gastric disturbance.

℞ Phosphori, gr. i.
   Alcohol absolut., q. s. ut dissolv.
   Glycerini, ad ℥ iv.
   Spts. menth. viridis, ℨ ss.
M.
Sig. One teaspoonful after eating, to be increased.

The phosphorated oil in capsules, or pills of pure phosphorus made up with bread crumbs, are good preparations, as is the combination of pure phosphorus and sulphur.

The actual cautery may be used with benefit in cases where there are well-defined painful points. A small platinum tip is to be employed, and the hyperæsthetic area whether it be in the scalp or elsewhere may be lightly touched. In cases of neuralgia of the great occipital this therapeutical measure is one of importance.

The bisulphide of carbon has been used as an external irritant. Gasparini has treated fifteen cases successfully, and his method is to apply to the painful point cotton-wool saturated with bisulphide. A few drops of the essence of peppermint will disguise the offensive odor.

External applications of ointments or liniments which contain anodyne substances sometimes do good, especially when there is much diffused hyperæsthesia. Among these are menthol, morphine, veratria, aconite, and belladonna; hypodermic injections of aconite, belladonna or daturia or osmic acid are at times beneficial.

An ointment containing morphine and veratria is sometimes excellent, and the following formula is recommended:

℞ Veratrinæ, gr. x.
Spts. vini recit., ♏xxx.
Morphinæ sulph., gr. xx.
Vaselini, ℥ ss.
M. Sig. For external use.

Bartholow recommends the oleate, and an ointment made up with benzoated lard.

"Oleatum veratrinæ:"

℞ Veratrine, 2 parts.
Oleic acid, 98 parts.
M.

"Unguentum veratrinæ:"

℞ Veratrine, 4 parts.
Alcohol, 6 parts.
Benzoinated lard, 96 parts.
M.

Very great care should be exercised in using these preparations as well as aconite embrocations, and the hands should always be washed after their application.

An ointment prepared by the combination of equal parts of chloral and camphor, with vaseline is a useful external application:

℞ Chloral hydrat.,
Camphoræ, ää ʒ ij.
Vaseline, ℥ ss.
M.

and we may add morphine to the prescription.

— 89 —

Various observers have used cocaine in neuralgia of the fifth nerve, both hypodermically and by application to the fauces and nasal fossæ. Papoff cured one bad case by local hypodermics of a 10 per cent. solution, using about half a syringe full. In one case of which I know when it was used by a dentist, and injected in the neighborhood of the inferior dental nerve, it produced facial paralysis, but I am unable to find others which contra-indicate its use. In some neuralgias due to catarrhal rhinitis, it promptly relieved the pain when it was used in the atomizer.

An excellent remedy in vogue in the country is a tincture made from the fruit of the belladonna. The berries should be crushed when green, and covered by strong alcohol. This makes a valuable external application.

Sclapiro* lays great stress upon the value of osmic acid. He cured five of eight cases and relieved the others. His formula is the following:

 ℞ Osmic acid, gr. 1·6.
  Distilled water, ℨ iss.
  Pure glycerin, ℨ j.
 M.

This preparation keeps two weeks, but without the glycerin readily decomposes. ♏v should be given hypodermically, and several injections are often necessary. Neuber has injected as much as 3 centigrammes

---

* Der Fortschritt, Dec., 5, 1885, No. 23.

of osmic acid within a period of three months without any bad results.

The use of cold obtained by means of the spray-producer is strongly advised. Some years ago I employed sulphuric ether for this purpose. The application should be made just in front of the ear over the painful points. 'The nasal injection of carbonic oxide, as recommended by Dupré and Brown-Sequard some years ago, is, I believe, a useless or at least unreliable mode of treatment.

Debove, Vinay, Peyronnet de Lafonville and Jacoby have all used with greater or less success the spray of methyl-chloride in the treatment of neuralgia of the fifth nerve. The primary results are freezing and anæsthesia, followed by redness and hyperæsthesia which subsides after a while, with a disappearance of the pain. An accident to be avoided is vesication.

I have devised a method of applying cold to a small territory which will often break up an attack of neuralgia. This consists of the adoption of a large felt-covered test tube, which is filled with finely-cracked ice and salt, or muriate of ammonia. An intense cold is produced, and the convex end, which is uncovered, may be applied to the sub-orbital foramen, or over any or all of the painful points in turn. The advantages over ether is the absence of danger where there are lights or fires, and of the odor of the latter, which often nauseates the patient.

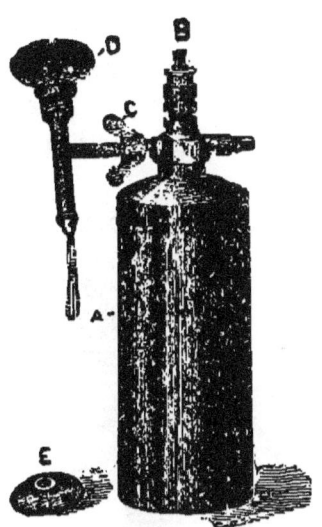

Fig. 5.
APPARATUS FOR USING METHYL-CHLORIDE.*

"In use, the direction of the spray having been determined by means of the thumb-screw C, a slight turn is made at B by means of the key E; this allows the vapor to pass into the tube connected with D; by turning D the amount and duration of the spray is regulated."

The treatment of neuralgic pains by vibrations as suggested by Mortimer Granville, Boudet and myself may be resorted to. The electrical apparatus devised by me, and afterwards modified by Boudet, may be employed. It is simply a flat piece of hard wood, on

---

* The above apparatus may be procured from Messrs. Mc Kesson & Robbins, of New York City.

which is mounted a vibrating tuning fork, actuated by a strong magnet. The current is supplied by a bichromate or other battery. The board is fitted with a projecting rod terminating in a knob which is

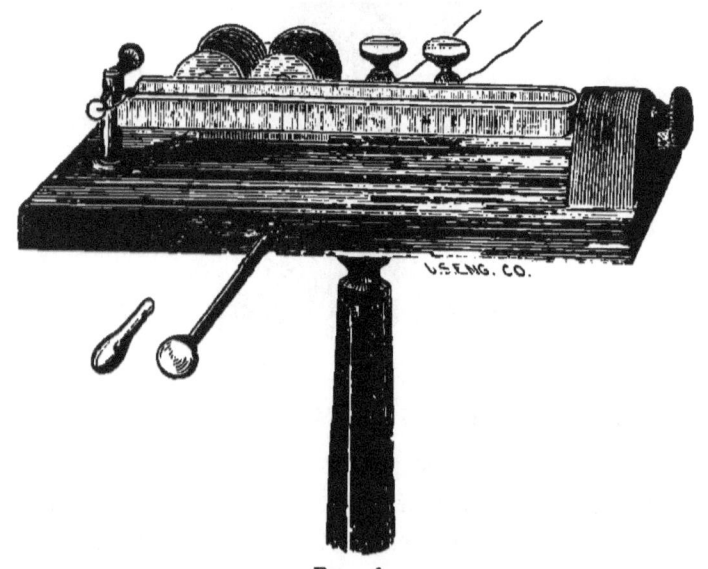

FIG. 6.

to be pressed against the painful point. When the current is connected the vibrations of the tuning fork are transmitted to the rod and in turn to the nerve. Though not uniformly beneficial, the use of the vibrator is often curative.*

---

*Also see reference to author's instrument and more extensive details in "Nervous Diseases, Their Description and Treatment." H. C. Lea's Sons & Co. Philadelphia. 1881. Second Edition.

Faradization or massage of the scalp are to be resorted to in severe cases with a decided prospect of

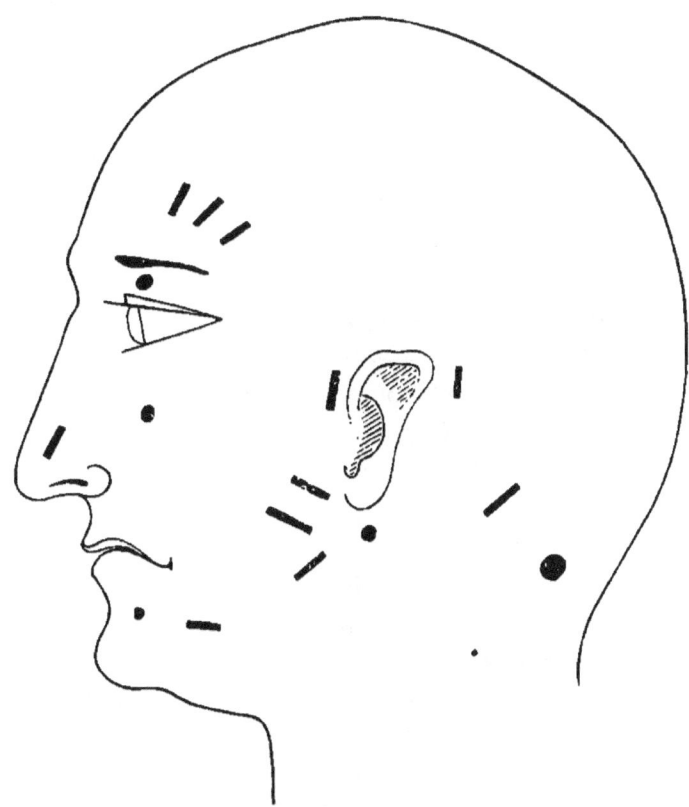

FIG. 7.
Points for electrization and cauterization of painful points.

benefit. The former, if not too strong, will soothe the patient, but if violent currents are applied there will be a decided aggravation of the pain of the neuralgia itself. A mild current passed through the hand of the operator—the patient holding one of the poles will often produce a feeling of drowsiness, and is followed by a subsidence of the paroxysm. The "wire brush" may be passed over the painful tracts.

In neuralgias of rheumatic origin when there are painful points, and tenderness which lasts several days, the use of an ordinary wire hair-brush with connections with the faradic battery; or light massage of the scalp (care being taken not to pull the hair), will be found to diminish the hyperæsthesia. In sub-occipital neuralgia faradization is highly efficacious.

The galvanic treatment of neuralgia of the fifth nerve is of immense importance, and it is generally recommended by the authorities upon nervous diseases. Small electrodes with sponge or chamois-covered heads are the best, or we may use a carbon-tipped electrode which may be covered with absorbent cotton. If currents of high tension or quantity are selected, it will be better to use an electrode with greater surface, otherwise we may cause intense pain when the smaller electrode is placed, as well perhaps as vesication. The cathodal electrode should be applied firmly on the tender points, and the anodal electrode just anterior to or below the ear. Currents that produce vertigo are to be avoided, and do no good. Daily applications of five or ten minutes duration are usually sufficient. In some cases the patient may be relieved by galvanization of the interior of the mouth.

For the relief of sub-occipital pain I have used nuchal applications of Gaiffe's revulsive disk with encouraging success.

Rosenthal has suggested the moist pack for one-half hour to an hour at a time in rheumatic cases, followed by galvanism. Static electricity, except in these cases, is of little or no use.

*Rasori, of Rome, has used the tuning fork in the treatment of neuralgia, applying it while vibrating over the course of the painful nerves.

The instrument was applied from 20 to 40 minutes. It also relieved nervous vomiting.

Tic douloureux (or prosopalgia) is best relieved by gelsemium—in fact I regard it as the best remedy at our disposal, but it must be given in large doses, and at least a mild toxic effect should be produced. From two to six or even eight minims should be the initial dose, and this may be increased. In the case of a medical friend who had taken an overdose by mistake, an epileptiform tic of several years standing was suddenly and completely cured by an overdose taken by mistake, which produced semi-collapse and many alarming symptoms. Croton chloral in twenty-grain doses sometimes does good, and Bramwell cured† a case by the use of drop doses of the one per cent. solution of nitro-glycerin thrice daily.

---

* The Journal of Nervous and Mental Diseases, Oct. 1, 1883.
† British Medical Journal 1884, p. 609.

*Dr. R. G. Simpson has reported a case where ice cap relieved tic douloureux when even morphine had failed.

Surgical measures are often necessary and may consist of traction, exsection, or those calculated to relive periostitis or disease of the antrum. Of the first of these I cannot speak in commendation, for the results are by no means permanent, and sometimes result in dangerous complications. A year or two ago it was a fashionable and sometimes successful operation. Lemaistre† has written fully upon his success, and details a number of experimental observations made by him with a view to determining the expenditure of force. A tension force equal to 8.83 lbs. was needed to stretch the nerve, and that there was never laceration of the gasserian ganglion, he explains by the protection afforded to this organ by the dura which covers it. Lemaistre prefers nerve stretching to the operation of Carnochan, which consists in breaking through the walls of the antrum.

Various other forms of nerve stretching have been suggested for prosopalgia. Ledentu has stretched the lingual nerve for a tic of five years standing, the nerve being elevated 12 mm. on a hook; and Polaillon has stretched the inferior dental, first trephining the inferior maxilla.

Nerve section is after all the only effectual method

---

* Cincinnati Lancet and Clinic, Oct. 20, 1883.
† Revue de Chirurgie, 1882, No. 12.

of curing obdurate neuralgia, but as many surgeons know, this operation affords only temporary relief unless it is extensive or thorough, and the following case of Richardson is an example in point. The first neurectomy was insufficient, the second effectual.

"Neuralgia of inferior dental nerve for five years. Division of nerve inside mouth; relief for two years. Return of pain in aggravated form, lasting one year. One inch of nerve destroyed by opening inferior dental canal from outside. Immediate recovery and cure.

"S. P. B., seventy-two years old, entered Sept. 3, 1886. Eight years ago, developed severe neuralgia in the right side of the face, over the lower jaw. Three years ago, inferior dental nerve was divided just above the point where it enters the dental foramen. This operation gave relief for two years, when the same trouble returned.

"August 4th. One inch of the inferior dental nerve was cut out. An incision parallel to, and through the fibres of the *masseter* muscle, three inches in length, was made down to the jaw-bone. With a gouge and mallet a narrow opening, one inch long, was made through the ramus of the jaw over the dental canal. The nerve and artery thus exposed were cut at each extremity of the opening, and the whole curetted out. There was little hæmorrhage. The external wound was closed with silk, and iodoform dressings applied.

"Two days later, stitches and drainage-tube were removed. For some days after the operation there was complaint of slight pain in the parts supplied by the mental branch of this nerve. This rapidly disappeared. He was discharged on the 10th.

"August 25th. Came and reported that 'it was a real pleasure to live; that he had had more real pleasure in life since leaving hospital than in any ten years before.'"

Epileptiform tic or prosopalgia has been cured by Perkovsky by division of the auriculo-temporal nerve. An incision ten centimeters long and five millimeters deep, should be made between the condyloid portion of the lower jaw and the anti-tragus.

Cadge* reports four cases of tic by neurectomy.

Richardson† in an admirable report upon neural operation, reports the following case of neurectomy for tic:

"Epileptiform neuralgia" of side of nose and face. Neurectomy of infra-orbital nerve; complete cure.

Tim O'Brien, sixty, married, laborer; entered hospital. August 8, 1885, with history of trouble in face for sixteen years. Some years ago had an operation done in an English hospital, without relief. Has pain in right side of face and nose, in parts supplied by the infra-orbital nerve. This is spasmodic, and

---

* British Medical Journal, July 15, 1882.
† Boston Medical and Surgical Journal, Oct. 21, 1886.

extends from the inner canthus of eye down to the ala of the nose. During this paroxysm he leans his head upon his hands, with evidence of great pain, and the muscles of the nose contract spasmodically upon the right side, drawing up the ala and wrinkling the skin.

August 12. Under ether, the infra-orbital nerve was found, a needle having been first inserted into the infra-orbital canal. The nerve was pulled out of the canal as far as possible, and cut. The peripheral end was then drawn up, and its branches dissected down an inch or more, and then divided.

The next day patient reported himself very comfortable, with pain much relieved. What pain still existed was referred to the ala of the nose.

August 18th. Five days after operation the pain had entirely left the face.

August 21st. No return of pain; face healed. Discharged.

In neuralgia of the inferior maxillary nerve, an infra-buccal operation is the easiest and best, and it may be divided just before it enters the dental canal.

Heustis* has cured a case of infra-orbital neuralgia by cutting down and exposing the infra-orbital foramen and drilling back as far as the spheno-maxillary fissure with a fine dentist's drill, thus removing the nerve.

Severe measures are often imperative, and re-

---
* Medical News, Dec. 8, 1883.

moval of Meckel's ganglion is an operation which often suggests itself.

Dr. Vanderveer* has cured two cases of infra-orbital neuralgia by removal of this ganglion. In one case the neuralgia remained absent for eight years. In another case there was no cure, and it was found that there was disease of one eye. However, when this was removed the patient recovered.

Dr. Vanderveer's first case and the operation therefor is the following:

"Miss B., aged 40, first consulted me July, 1875, giving the following history. For three or four years previous she had suffered from neuralgic pains in right side of the face, differing as to length of time and degree of severity. Her general health up to this time had been good. Passed the menopause about two years before. Since that time she had had little relief from pain unless under the influence of medicine. All her teeth had been removed (one or two at a time) from right side upper jaw, and some from the lower jaw on that side, with but little, if any, relief resulting. Had taken medicines almost constantly. For the previous six months she had had no remission of pain, though taking large doses of morphine, chloral and bromides. The pain would start in the upper jaw, extend over the face, pass down, around and through the lower, to chin and along right side of tongue, also penetrating the temporal

---

* N. Y. Medical Record, June 9, 1883.

region, leaving a heat or inflammation in the mouth, very severe.

"At times she would be unable to take a drink without having the pain aggravated for hours.

"I gave her large doses precip. carb. iron; also Brown-Sequard's neuralgic pills, but with no apparent benefit. Gave hypodermic injections chloroform with a few moments' respite from pain, but the inflammation following was very severe. Also gave morphine in the same manner, but so little good followed that she readily consented to an operation.

"On September 5, 1875, ether being given, I proceeded to remove the infra-orbital nerve and Meckel's ganglion in the following manner: Making an incision from the right angle of the eye, down to the bone, along the nerve at a distance of little more than an inch; then another incision, similar in length, at right angles, under the infra-orbital ridge, raising the flap and periosteum, I exposed enough of the anterior wall of the antrum to admit the application of a good-sized trephine, removing a button of bone, so that the upper edge, opening, exposed the infra-orbital nerve and its canal. Lifting the nerve from its bed by means of a bone chisel, grooved director and probe, I followed it until the posterior wall of antrum was reached, where, by means of a smaller trephine, another button of bone was removed, and the spheno-palatine fossa reached. The ganglion was now lifted from its bed and, with curved scissors, the nerve and it were severed and removed. This was followed by a sharp hæmorrhage, and at first somewhat alarming, but controlled by portions of sponge, firmly applied, to which a silk ligature had been tied. The wound in the face was then closed by interrupted sutures, a drainage tube, with ligature from sponge, being placed in most dependent point. The patient rallied nicely from the anæsthetics, and was immediately relieved from all pain. There was considerable trouble in re-

FIG. 8.

moving the sponge, and the parts suppurated quite a good deal, but ultimately healed kindly. From that time on she has been in perfect health, increasing in flesh, attending fully to her work, and a more grateful patient I have never seen.   *   *   *   *

By taking out a good-sized button from the posterior wall of the antrum, and watching carefully, the internal maxillary artery can be seen pulsating, and thus avoided, while a most excellent view of the ganglion can be obtained. As with all operations upon the nerves, I am convinced the operation needs to be done thoroughly; if not, failure is likely to result, as it will, in cases where the pathological lesion is still more central and the cause not peripheral. In lifting the infra-orbital nerve from its bony canal, I found, in my last operation, the instrument here shown figured of great service, as by its use the operator is not so likely to tear or separate the nerve—something very important to avoid, for, by keeping the nerve in its continuity, he has a sure and safe guide to and along the ganglion."

In a patient with stubborn neuralgia of the inframaxillary branch of the nerves, Hach found a large granulation at the back of the pharynx, and when this was cauterized the patient's pain left almost as by magic. It cannot be questioned that disease of the nasal fossa, or middle ear troubles are at the bottom of many neuralgias.

Gross* has described a form of neuralgia, met with chiefly in elderly persons who have lost their teeth. It is confined chiefly to the upper jaw, and depends upon a low grade of periositis with deposits of bony material and pressure of the smaller nerve filiaments.

Some neuralgias may be cured by empirical means, and that reported by Durham is one in point. Durham vainly tried to relieve an inveterate supra-orbital neuralgia by stretching the superior branch; only temporary comfort was obtained, but when the trephine was applied over a cicatrix upon one side of the head, which had been left by the kick of a horse, it was found that an immediate cure was effected.

---

* Am. Journal of Med. Science, vol. lv, 1870, p. 48.

The simple excision of old cicatrices is often imperative, even when no bone disease is suspected, but when there is periositis and necrosis, it is absolutely necessary to resort to appropriate surgical measures.

CHAPTER VI.

NEURASTHENIC HEADACHES.

Under this head comes a long list of irregular headaches of obscure causation, but dependent more or less upon conditions of neural weakness. The headaches of neurasthenia include some already spoken of as anæmic. They have oftentimes an hysterical element, or depend upon reflex mischief. Oculists have for a long time recognized the headache from eye-strain; gynæcologists, those from ovarian and uterine disorders.

Hysterical headaches are likely to be of the most varied description, and but one form is at all characteristic, that known as *clavus hystericus*. This consists of an intense and localized head-pain, which has been compared to that which might follow the driving a nail into the head. It is nearly always vertical. Hysterical women are very apt to complain of very great diffused hyperæsthesia of the scalp, so that the simple act of brushing the hair causes great distress. All hysterical headaches are worse at the catamenial periods, and are aggravated by fatigue, excitement, late hours, etc. There is often attendant ovarian irritation or backache, and much mental irritability. The pain of clavus is rather intractable, and actual resources to the hypodermic injection of morphine and atropine is sometimes absolutely necessary. These patients are more apt than any others to form the opium habit, or that of alcoholism, and great care should be taken lest, by yielding to their demands, we foster something worse than the headache or hysteria.

External applications of the wire brush with mild faradic currents will often mitigate the suffering, and should this fail, we may resort to the ether spray. Massage to the head is recommended by Webber, but it is by no means agreeable to all patients. The citrate of caffeine or bromide of caffeine are often serviceable. Valerinate of ammonia and cypripedin are also useful. The latter may be used in the form of the fluid extract, and dram doses frequently repeated will be found to increase the patient's comfort.

The following formula is recommended:

℞ Ammon carbonas, ʒ iij.
    Tr. moschi, ʒ vj.
    Spts. lavandulæ, ʒ i.
    Elixir ammon valerianas, ad ℥ viij.
M.
Two teaspoonsful at a dose, in water.

A rectal injection of half an ounce of the tincture assafœtida in a pint of thin starch water will not only help these headaches, but is useful in other hysterical troubles, notably those of a convulsive nature. Most patients of this kind need iron and it may be given in combination with small quantities of the hydrochlorate of cocaine.

    ℞ Cocaini hydrochlor., gr. iv.
       Ferri et strychniæ citras, gr. xxiv.
       Ext. gentianæ, gr. xlviii.
    M Ft. massæ et divid in pillulæ, No. xxiv.
    Sig. One after each meal.

The iodide of iron is often more serviceable than any other preparation especially in combination with Calumbo.

Great good results from the application of the actual cautery, or blisters over the ovaries, and in many cases the left ovary will be found hyperæsthetic.

The headaches of exhaustion have been alluded to before under the head of cerebral hyperæmia. It remains for me to call attention to a variety which bears no relation to the condition of emptiness or fulness of the blood-vessels of the brain—a headache, in fact, with exhaustion of the nerve cells. Such a cephalalgia always follows unusual fatigue, be it mental or physical; is occasionly frontal, but more often vertical, and is neither paroxysmal or sharp. It disappears sometimes quite promptly after a glass of whiskey and water, or champagne; or a good night's rest. The faculties are often pre-naturally active, and the individual is mentally hyperæsthetic. He may have insomnia, but his sleeplessness is of the quiet kind, and he simply lies wide awake and there is no tossing, heat of head, or anxiety. The surface of the body may be cold and the face pale.

Diffusible stimulants bring relief as does the "phosphoric acid lemonade," which may be made by the addition of a few drops of lemon juice and a lump of sugar to a half teaspoonful of dilute phosphoric acid and a tumblerful of water. A new preparation, the benzoate of sodium and caffeine, may be given in five to fifteen grain doses hourly. Guarana or the fluid extract of paullina sorbilis in tablespoonful doses. Cocaine in doses of one-half of a grain. Strong coffee or green tea are excellent abortants of an attack of headache of the kind. Wurm has given quinine or morphine in combination with guarana with excellent effect. In the cases where it is useful, dry heat to the head is more agreeable than cold or ice compresses. A glass of very dry champagne, or a teaspoonful or two of absinthe which have been poured over finely cracked ice, are also recommended.

The most efficacious preparations for continuous treatment are those of the restorative class. A pill of the arseniate of strychnine, strophanthus and quinine is recommended.

℞ Strychnine arsenias, gr. ss,
Sem. strophanthii pulv., gr. vi,
Quinæ sulph., gr. xlviii.

Ft massæ et divid in pillulæ No. xlviii.
M. Sig.—One to two after each meal.

A stimulating preparation of iron may be suggested, and I know of none better than the ethereal acetate. This may be given alone or in combination with strychnine.

    ℞ Strychniæ acetas, gr. ss—gr. i,
        Tr. ferri acet ether, 3 vi,
        Aquæ lauro cerasi, ℥ iv.
    M.—One teaspoonful after eating in water.

Iron and ignatia, perhaps in combination with arsenic may be prescribed with advantage.

    ℞ Ignatiæ,
        Acidi arseniosi, ää gr. i,
        Ferri redacti,
        Ext. gentianæ, ää gr. xl.
    F t massæ et divid. in pillulæ No. xl.
    M.—One after each meal.

Besides iron, we may make use of one of the preparations of phosphorus before enumerated.

Burgess* recommends the use of aconite for the treatment of the headache of exhaustion, and it may be used mainly in small repeated doses of one or two minims until relief is obtained.

General hygienic measures, such as bathing and massage, head shampooing, and rest as far as possible; change of scene and air are necessary and important adjuvants.

Certain vague headaches have been called

---

*Edinburgh Medical and Surgical Journal, 1840, p. 95-105.

"sympathetic." The application of this term must lead to confusion, for little or no attention is paid to the actual pathological state. The same fault may be found with the term "nervous." All practical men recognize the existence of irregular headaches from gastric, hepatic, or visceral disorders generally, and each case must be studied from a different standpoint, and the individual indications properly met and overcome.

Various remote disturbances which tax nervous energy to its utmost, or a constant, remote, and often unsuspected irritation are productive of these headaches. In women they are closely related to the menstrual periods, or with the condition of the digestive organs. Following upon the ingestion of rich or improper food they symptomatise a gastric irritation. Some people call them "bilious," though the function of the liver may in every way be normal.

I have already alluded to a form of headache in which ovarian irritation plays a part, and in such cases it is not unusual to find leucorrhœa, backache, coldness and clamminess of the hands, insomnia, palpitation and muscular feebleness.

The so-called "bilious" or stomachic headache usually affects individuals who present epigastric uneasiness, eructations of acid fluids, sudden hunger which is easily appeased. "sinking" sensations, cardiac distress, flatulence; and a decided atony of the bowels which is manifested by alternating constipation and looseness. The stools are not well formed. Iced or very hot drinks taken into the stomach often produce immediate head pain which is frontal, and an acute attack of indigestion is the origin of a reflex headache which may be vertical, and not attended by any signs of disturbed cerebral circulation.

A cause of "sympathetic" headaches originates in the irritation from bad teeth which need not necessarily produce neuralgia, and the reflex irritation attendant upon the appearance of the wisdom teeth often gives rise to headaches of a diffused and almost constant character, which only ceases with complete dentition. Aural disease is perhaps a more common cause of headache than we imagine. It may, or not be attended by tinnitus, but often is by vertigo, which may be general or lateral. Not only may disease of the organs of hearing produce a neuralgia or a headache which affects the side of the head and is dull and accompanied by tenderness, but there is a reflected irritation which may be the starting point of a genuine sympathetic headache.

Besides the proper surgical or mechanical measures, such as operation, syringing, etc., we may administer strychnine in large doses, or belladonna. I have had unusual success with the latter drug pressed to the point of tolerance. The removal of a plug of wax will sometimes cure headaches that have defied many remedies, and warm syringing will decidedly ameliorate the patient's suffering.

Dr. Harrison Allen, of Philadelphia, has called the attention of the profession to a purely nervous headache due to catarrhal disease of the nose. The pain he considers reflex, and it is confined to the side of the head and face and sometimes the vertex. Wood says that the patient can often define it by "drawing the index finger across the face from the middle of the nose to the temple, and thence in some cases to the parietal eminence." Sometimes the pain resembles migraine and is associated with nausea.

It has been the fashion of late to ascribe to disorders of accommodation and refraction, not only many forms of headache, but other nervous disorders as well, such as epilepsy and chorea. Certain disingenuous or ignorant persons have even claimed to cure posterior spinal sclerosis, and degeneration of the pyramidal columns of the spinal cord by ocular myotomy; and all manner of extreme operative interference, which smacks strongly of charlatanism, has been indulged in.

The existence of headaches due to eye-strain has been recognized for years by those who have made the eyes a study, and the provision of proper glasses and treatment calculated to improve the tone of the ocular muscles has often been promptly followed by substantial relief. The location and character of pain vary greatly, but as a rule the former is either suboccipital or frontal. Some ophthalmologists ascribe the sub-occipital pain to accommodation weakness, and the frontal headache to refractive disturbance, but others are equally sure there is no constancy in the connection. The headache of eye-strain is of course produced by reading, and aggravated by persistent use of the eyes, and by bright lights. It is dull and continuous, and may be accompanied by lachrymation and photophobia.

Hypermetropic persons are those who most often suffer from headaches of this character, and with the hypermetropia there is often considerable astigmatism. Myopic persons, through injudicious use of their eyes, also suffer from dull, persistent vertigo and a great deal of distress. The victims of ocular headaches, as a rule, have red swollen eyes, and when the inner surface of the lids is exposed, there will be found a low grade of inflammation with granulation. Through insufficiency of the recti, a variety of muscular asthenopia occurs with headaches. This is developed by close application to fine work, and obstinately resists ordinary treatment. After the patient's power of ocular adduction or abduction is determined by means of prisms, a pair of concave glasses may be selected, or prisms may be provided to overcome the weakness of the recti. In hypermetropic headaches, convex glasses are indicated, and at first those of low power may be provided, which are to be afterwards increased.

Some observers have noted a variety of migraine, which is due to eye-strain and differs but little from the common forms, except, perhaps, that it is more localized.

There is a form of headache from mechanical vibration which is neurasthenic, and I have met with it among railroad men or machinists. It is diffused, present a great deal of the time, and attended by mental hyperæsthesia. When it is possible the patient should be made to discontinue his work and seek rest, but if this cannot be done, the treatment should consist in cerebral sedatives, the bromides ranking first.

INDEX.

	PAGE.
Ability to Locate Pain	2
Acetanilid	46
Aconite in Neuralgia	83
Actual Cautery	87, 107
Alcohol	28
Alcoholic Headache	6
Alkaline Baths	11
Ammonia, Valerianate of	106
Anæmic Headaches	52
Rest Treatment in	52
Angio-Paretic Migraine	20
Angio-Spastic Migraine	35
Antifibrine	46
Antipyrine in Neuralgia	84
Antipyrine	46
Antrum, Disease of	82
Arseniate of Strychnine	108
Assafœtida	106
Aural Disease as Cause of Headache	111
Bad Teeth	46, 111
Baths, Alkaline	11
Baths, Needle	26
Benham on Cold	28
Benzoate of Sodium and Caffeine	108
Betol	50
Bromide of Ammonium	35
Bilious Headache	110

	PAGE.
Caffeine Bromide	106
Citrate	106
Caffeinic headache	76
Cannabis Indica	35
Case, Vulpian's	82
Cerebral Anæmia of Aged People,	44
Chloride of Ammonium	85
Chloroform	12
Classification of Headaches	3
Clavus Hystericus	105
Cocaine	108
Cod-Liver Oil	14
Congestive Headaches	5
Causes of	7, 8
Symptoms of	5
Cold, Benham on	28
in Neuralgia	90
Corning's Method	30
Connection of Visual Defects	113
Cracked ice	90
Croton Chloral	84
Cypripedin	106
Diet in Anæmic Headaches	44
Lithæmic Headache	67
Diabetic headache	75
Division of Inferior Dental Nerve	98
Donovan's Solution	86
Duquesnel's Solution	84
Epileptiform Tic, Division of Auriculo-Temporal Nerve in.	98
Ergotin	17
Ergot	16
Excision of Cicatrix in Neuralgia	103, 104

	PAGE.
Excretion of Uric Acid in Gouty Headache	67
Exhaustion	107
Eye Strain as Cause of Headache	112
Faradization, General	53
Facial Neuralgia	78
Formula for Osmic Acid Injection	89
Fothergill in Regard to Anæmic Headache	34
Fothergill's Solution	23
Fork, the Tuning	95
Gaiffe's Disk	95
Galvanism	30, 94
Gouty Headache	67
Gas, Nitrous Oxide	39
Oxygen	39
Gout, Quiet	68
Haig on Diet	67
Hæmophilia as Cause of Anæmic Headache	36
Headache, Alcoholic	6
Aural Disease as a Cause of	111
Bad Teeth as a Cause of	111
Bilious	110
Bitter Tonics in	6
Bromides in	12
Brain-work as a Cause of	7
Caffein in	76
Canabis Indica in	35
Cerebral Surgery for Relief of	64
Cholæmic	71
Cerebral Tumor a Cause of	60
Classification of	3
Diabetic	75
Digitalis in	7

	PAGE.
Headache, Defective Hygienic Conditions a Cause of	31
From Debauch	5
Gouty	65
Heat	7
Hysterical	105
Ice-bags for Relief of	7
Isolation as a Cause of	7
Lithæmic	65
Location of	2
Malarial	74
Meningeal	59
Naphthalol in Treatment of	50
Nasal	112
Nervous	110
Neuralgic	78
Neurasthenic	105
Of Exhaustion	107
Of Menopause	23
Of Meningitis	17
Of Lithæmia	65
Operations on Ocular Muscles for Relief of	112
Organic	55
Ovarian	105, 110
Pathology of	1
Sexual	24
Sick	21
Sub-occipital	8
Toxæmic	65
Uterine	2
Uræmic	71
Varieties of	1
Veratrum Viride in	7
Vibratory	113
Anæmic	33

	PAGE.
Headache, Anæmic Absinthe in	43
Albuminate of Iron in	38
Cases of	33
Chartreuse in	43
Citrate of Caffeine in	49
Cocaine in	41
Fothergill on	34
General Faradization in	53
Hypophosphites in	40
Injection of Dried Blood in	54
Iron in	39
Marshall Hall on	45
Metrorrhagia in	34
Nasal Stenosis as a Cause of	44
Nitrous Oxide Gas in	50
Opium in	42
Symptoms of	33
Strychnia in	39
Congestive	5
Alcohol in	28
Arsenic in	16
Cardiac Hypertrophy	14
Climate for	32
Cod-liver Oil in	14
Diet in	26
Galvanism in	30
Ergot in	16
Meat Diet Harmful in	14
Meningeal	17
Mercurials for	15, 16
Phosphates in	10
Pressure	29
Pulse in	15
Symptoms of	5

	PAGE.
Headache, Congestive, Turkish Baths in	24
Conjestive	5
Alcoholic	5
Alkaline Baths in	11
Aperient Water in	6
Bromides in	6
Camphor in	9
Cupping in	12
Cutaneous Revulsion in	9
Exposure to Sun, from	7
In Anæmic Patients	7
Packing	12
Purgatives in	15
Veratrum Viride in	7
Head Evil	105
Head Symptoms	110
Herpes in Neuralgia	81
Hydrencephaloid Condition	45
Hungarian Waters	25
Hunyadi Janos Water	25
Hysterical Headache	105
Infra-orbital Neuralgia	78
Intra-cranial Neuralgia	81
Introduction	1
Insolation, in Cases of	7
Iodoform	49
Iron, Albuminate of	38
Koumyss	52
Liniments	30
Lithæmic Headaches	65
Lemaire Picquot on Arsenic	16
Left Ovary, Hyperæsthenia of	107

	PAGE.
Lemonade, Phosphoric Acid	108
Localization of Head Pain	2
Malarial Headaches	74
Malate of Iron	37
Massage of Scalp	93
Matzoon	52
Meckel's Ganglion, Removal of	100
Methyl Chloride	90
Meningeal Congestive Headache	17
Meningitis, Headache of	59
Migraine	19
Ammonia Muriate in	22
Angio-paretic	20
Angio-spastic	35
Association with Epilepsy	20
Bromo-caffein in	22
Bromides in	22
Coffee in	22
Chloral in	22
of Children	46
Routh's Formula	23
Symptoms of	20
Treatment of	22
Mortimer Granville's Apparatus	91
Nasal Bleeding	18
Nasal Headache	112
Nasal Stenosis	44
Needle Bath	26
Neuralgia, Aconite in	83
Actual Cautery in	87
Ammoniated Copper in	85
Antipyrin and Antifebrin in	84
Belladonna in	87

	PAGE.
Neuralgia, Bi-sulphide of Carbon in	87
Chloride of Ammonia in	85
Chloride of Methyl in	90
Cimicifuga in	85
Cocaine in	87
Croton Chloral in	84
Divisions of	78
Division of Infra-dental Nerve in	98
Donovan's Solution in	86
Electricity, Static in	95
Ether Spray in	90
Frontal	78
Gaiffe's Disk in	95
Galvanism in	94
General Treatment of	85
Herpes in	81
Intra-cranial	81
Local Treatment of	87
Methyl Chloride in	90
Moist Pack in	95
Neuro-Paralytic Ophthalmia in	81
Nerve Stretching in	96
Nitrous Oxide Gas	39
Ointment for	87
Osmic Acid in	89
Phosphorus in	86
Refrigeration in	90
Supra Orbitral	79, 81
Sub-occipital	86
Tonga in	85
Trophic Disease in	81
Tr. Actea Rac in	85
Use of Cold in	90
Veratria in	87
Vibratory Treatment of	91

	PAGE.
Neurasthenic Headaches	105
Nervous Headaches	110
Ointments	87
Organic Headaches, Belladonna in	59
Diagnosis of	55
Ergot in	59
Ether Evaporation in	59
Head Coil in	58
Operation on Eyes for Cure of Headache	112
Osmic Acid Injection	89
Ovarian Headache	105
Phosphorus	86
Pathology of Headache	1
Percenter	92
Percussion of Skull	62
Periostitis of Alveolar Process as Cause	103
Phosphorus, Thompson's Solution of	87
Phosphoric Acid Lemonade	108
Pharyngeal Granulation as Cause of Neuralgia	103
Physostigma	11
Prosopalgia	98
Purgation	25
Quiet Gout	68
Rectal Injections of Assafœtida	106
Dried Blood	54
Salicylate of Soda	69
Salol	70
Scalp, Faridization of	93
School Children, Headache of	12
Sick Headache	21
Sexual Headache	24

	PAGE.
Solution, Fothergill's	23
Routh's	23
Springs, Mineral	24, 25
Strophanthus	108
Strychnine, Arseniate of	108
Supra-Orbital Neuralgia	81
Surgery Cerebral	64
Sympathetic Headache	110
Syphilitic Headache	56
Large Doses of Iodide in	57
Tic Douloureaux	95
Gelsemium in	95
Nitro-glycerin in	95
Neurectomy in	98
Nerve Stretching in	96
Tonga	85
Toxæmic Headache	65
Tobacco as Cause of	76
Trigeminal Neuralgia	78
Trophic Disorders in Neuralgia	81
Tumor as Cause of Headache	60
Uræmic Headache	71
Symptoms of	71
Diet in	72
Tri-Nitrine in	73
Use of Cold	28
Ophthalmoscope in Diagnosis of Headache	62
Valerianate of Ammonia	106
Vulpian's Case	82
Wax in the Ear as Cause	111
Wire Brush	94
Woakes on Headache	8

www.ingramcontent.com/pod-product-compliance
Lightning Source LLC
Chambersburg PA
CBHW020113170426
43199CB00009B/521